Marsha,
Hope you enjoy the book,
Thanks for reading!

Marty Gallagher

THE TEACHER

Mom's Powerful Lessons in Her Final Days

Marty Gallagher

Angier Publishing

The Teacher

Mom's Powerful Lessons in Her Final Days

©2021 Marty Gallagher

print ISBN: 978-1-09836-703-9
ebook ISBN: 978-1-09836-704-6

DEDICATION

This book is dedicated to my five children, Carly, Molly, Ben, Sophie and Leo. Molly and Ben were only eight and five years old when their Grandma Gallagher died on January 9, 2009. Carly and Sophie came into my life two months later, when I met their mother – and the love of my life – Emily. After Emily and I were later married, Leo was born in 2014.

To this day, it makes me sad that Emily, Carly, Sophie and Leo never had a chance to meet my mom. One of the main reasons for writing this book is to introduce her to them.

I want Emily and each of our children to appreciate my mom's intelligence, wisdom, strength, sense of humor, faith, optimism and selfless nature. I know she watches over them now and loves them all. I hope they continue to make her proud. I know they will.

This book is also dedicated to my seven siblings (Maggie, Dan, Joe, Tim, Katie, Ed and Jerry), and my 22 nieces and nephews. My siblings and I share the wonderful bond of growing up in a small Iowa town called Strawberry Point (population 1,400), in a four-bedroom house with 10 people. We didn't have an abundance of luxuries, but we never wanted for anything. We had a big yard, siblings to play with, and two parents who encouraged us to try different things and always do our best.

We have different personalities and interests, but my siblings and I share one important thing in common: We were raised by wonderful, caring and supportive parents. We learned to share, we learned patience, we learned to look after each other, we learned to respect authority, we learned to handle success and failure, and we learned the importance of laughter.

We also saw first-hand how loving parents raise their children. I think we have each taken those lessons and applied them to our own families as adults. In my view, that has worked out pretty well. I know I'm extremely biased, but I think my nieces and nephews are among the most amazing young people I've ever met.

—————————

Finally, this book is dedicated to my parents.

While the focus of this book is my mom and the many lessons she taught us, my dad is one of the most intelligent, successful, driven and kind-hearted people I've ever known. He is 96 years old now and it has been more than 12 years since my mom died. Dad misses her every day.

One thing that consistently lifts his spirits, though, is sharing stories about Mom. It makes him happy whether he's telling the stories or hearing them from someone else. I think there's a common misconception that people have when they know somebody who has lost a loved one. They might be uncomfortable talking about the person who has died, so they avoid the topic altogether when talking to a surviving family member. People rationalize this as a way "to keep the person from feeling bad." The reality is that it may have the opposite effect.

Hearing a story about Mom, whether it's heartwarming or funny, makes my dad feel *better*, not worse. It lets him know that other people are thinking of her too and that other people know how much he cared about her. It reminds him of the impact she had on so many people. And I think, in a way, it lets Dad know that people aren't simply forgotten after they're gone.

I like the idea of writing a book about Mom because she absolutely LOVED books. My mom would read one book per day, whether it was a 200-page murder mystery or a 400-page biography. She loved to read, she loved a good story, and she knew more things about a wide variety of topics than anyone I've known.

I always told Mom she would be a fantastic game-show contestant because she was so well-read. She would smile and shake her head. Being the center of attention was never her thing, so from that angle, Mom would not like being the focal point of a book.

But I know this much: Mom would read it. Cover to cover, in one day.

Hopefully, some of her grandchildren will read this book and in doing so, they will get to know Grandma Gallagher a little better, feel a sense of pride in who she was (and who they are) and possibly learn one or two of her favorite lessons along the way. Maybe someday, their children will do the same.

I think Mom would like that.

CONTENTS

INTRODUCTION

Carly, Molly, Ben, Sophie and Leo,

I am writing this book for you. I don't know how old you'll be when you sit down to read it, but I hope it will have a positive impact on you.

Your Grandma Gallagher was a wonderful, strong, patient and intelligent woman with a big heart and the best laugh. She was a tremendous influence on who you are, both directly and indirectly, and you should be extremely proud to know who she was.

I want you to know that she lived an extraordinary life, affecting thousands of lives around her in a positive way through her work in education. I want you to know she was a phenomenal parent to her eight children and that she juggled responsibilities all day long, showing a terrific sense of humor through it all. I want you to know she was a woman with a very strong faith in God and she prayed constantly. I want you to know she was Grandpa Gallagher's best friend and they loved each other completely throughout 47 years of marriage.

I want you to know these things because I love you with all my heart. I know Grandma Gallagher would be embarrassed to read some of the things you will read in this book, but I also know she would laugh out loud, shake her head, and read it over and over again.

I miss Grandma every day.

But I know she lived a happy life. I know she was so proud of her children and grandchildren. I know she loved Grandpa Gallagher. I know she was passionate about her work and, as a result, didn't feel like she ever had "a job." I know she had an infectious, loud laugh. I know she loved a good story. I know she could cram 25 hours of work into each day without complaint. I know she would suffer quietly. I know that with a simple look on her face, she could make me want to do better. I know she could make me feel proud of myself with her smile. I know she always cared so much more about the happiness and comfort of those around her than she cared about her own feelings.

I want *you* to know these things, too.

Grandma Gallagher was a teacher. Whether she was making supper for a family of 10 people, or reading a book to a classroom of kindergartners, she was always teaching. Sometimes, she would spell out the lesson very clearly and other times, I would pick up on the lesson by watching how she handled certain situations.

I learned a great deal from her, more than I can list for you in these pages. I simply want to share with you some of the things Grandma Gallagher taught me that have stuck with me through the years. And I want you to be able to learn from her actions, as well.

The best way I can illustrate who Grandma Gallagher was is to share with you some stories about the final 12 days of her life, with several other anecdotes mixed in, and the lessons she was still teaching in her final days and hours. Even with her last breath.

I hope you enjoy this book. I hope it teaches you some things about Grandma Gallagher you didn't know. I hope it also makes you laugh out loud, shake your head, and that you read it over and over again.

THE
TEACHER

CHAPTER 1

MONDAY, DECEMBER 29, 2008

"In life, there are no *do overs*." That was one of my mom's favorite sayings. And of course, it's true. However, I really wish I had a second chance at getting things right on Monday, December 29, 2008.

That evening, I make plans to go out to eat with two of my good friends, Ben Dvergsten and Mike Kohler, in our hometown of Storm Lake, Iowa (population 10,000). We go to The Regatta Grille, a new restaurant down by the lake. A couple of our old buddies, Matt Wilson and Aaron Brock, are in town and join us.

I am 39 years old. It has been 14 years since I was Matt's and Aaron's high school basketball coach, and it is a rarity for them to be in town. Matt lives in Florida and Aaron lives in California, so I haven't had the chance to visit with them in a few years. I look forward to seeing them, telling some old stories, catching up on new tales and laughing.

My cell phone rings about halfway through dinner, around 7:30 p.m. It's my dad. He tells me he had taken Mom to the hospital late this afternoon and the doctors are going to "keep her overnight for tests." My parents also live in Storm Lake, about four blocks from my house. Dad is 84 years old and Mom is 72. I am the only one of my seven siblings who live in this small town too, so we spend a lot of time together and are very close.

Dad sounds calm, but I know that Mom hasn't been feeling well, so I ask if he wants me to come to the hospital to join them.

Dad scoffs at that notion, saying, "No, no, no. You have dinner with your friends. She would not be happy if you skipped that to come here. She's going to be sleeping anyway. They just need to get some fluids in her." I know Mom has been feeling sick for about nine days, ever since my siblings and their families left Storm Lake on Sunday, December 21 after we all celebrated Christmas together. Mom has had very little energy and hasn't been eating much.

It makes sense the doctor wants to have her stay overnight, get some nutrition in her and help get her energy back. I want to believe that's all Mom needs and she will be on her way back home sometime tomorrow. Deep down, I probably know better.

Despite Dad's resistance, I think I should go to the hospital anyway. I feel I should be there. But I don't go. I should listen to my gut. Instead, I stay at the restaurant and enjoy the dinner with my friends.

It's the one regret I have during Mom's last two weeks.

Mom didn't get to go back home the next day. In fact, she never made it back home at all. Today was actually the beginning of the end, which is something I didn't want to realize, or even consider, at that moment.

The Lesson: Your actions speak louder than words. I know Mom would have bristled at the notion of me skipping dinner with my old friends to come to the hospital that night. But I also know, if the roles had been reversed, she would've been there for me. Just like she had been a million times before.

I may not have been able to help in any practical way that night, so Dad was probably right about that. But, in the end, simply "being there" for someone, showing your support and your love in that way, speaks volumes. I know Mom didn't have any issue with it, but I also know that I disappointed myself with my choice that night. Unfortunately, in life, there are no "do overs."

———————

I coached boys basketball at Storm Lake High School from the fall of 1992 through the spring of 2000. The first two years, I was the junior varsity head coach and varsity assistant coach. The last six years, I was the varsity head coach.

During those winter months of December, January and February, we played our games in small Iowa towns like Estherville, LeMars, Spencer and Hull. Our typical road game was approximately 75 miles from Storm Lake. The weather in Iowa is unpredictable in any season, but this is especially true in the winter, when snow, wind, sleet and ice can make travel difficult and at times, dangerous. During my eight seasons as a basketball coach, my teams played a total of 206 games.

Mom attended every one of those games. *Every. Single. One.*

Don't get me wrong. She didn't see this as an enormous sacrifice. Mom loved sports. She would sit in the stands and cheer as loudly as anyone else. Mom would also always have a scorebook with her, keeping track of each player's points and fouls in basketball … and each at-bat in baseball.

But I know that as much as she enjoyed the games, she wasn't going to let anything stop her from getting there because she wanted to support me. Regardless of the weather, the forecast or the distance, my parents would be there.

During the summer months when I was growing up, there were usually three or four of the six Gallagher boys in Little League. It was fairly typical for Mom to spend three hours of a summer afternoon sitting in the bleachers, watching her elementary-aged boys play baseball. Then, we would go home and she would get those dirty uniforms in the laundry, make supper for our family of 10 people, and then head back to our high school field to watch one or two of the older boys play for our high school team.

When she would get home that night, she would surely finish the laundry, including the Little League uniforms, and get more started, including the high school uniforms. While doing all those things, Mom was also in charge of keeping every kid on time to get where we were supposed to be, making sure we had food on the table and stopping us from picking on each other to a degree that it would drive anyone crazy.

With eight children, there was a never-ending amount of laundry to do, grocery shopping to complete, clothes to patch up, meals to prepare and arguments to officiate. I assume Mom also needed to catch her own breath from time to time and possibly have a thought or two unrelated to making lunch, doing laundry or being the Chief Disciplinarian.

But she never missed a game. She never missed a school play, musical, concert or any other performance that her children were participating in, either. Mom was always there, showing her support and quick with words of encouragement.

The Lesson: Support your family in whatever they do. The support you show someone with your words is a good thing, but nothing beats the support you show someone with your actions. Everyone is busy and there are always reasons to NOT do something. Make it a priority to show support for your family with your actions.

One Friday afternoon in April 2005, I was out for a walk with my two-year-old son Ben. I was 35 years old. It was a beautiful spring day, about 65 degrees and breezy, the type of day Mom would call "sweatshirt weather." Ben and I were about two blocks from my house, on a sidewalk in front of our middle school.

Mom drove up beside us in her little, dark red, 2002 Malibu. She pointed at me to open the passenger-side door, so I did.

"Get in," Mom said to me.

I looked at her funny and, knowing this was very unusual from her, I asked, "Why? What's going on?"

"Just get in," Mom said in a tone of voice that I rarely heard from her, but one that clearly meant she was serious. "I want to talk to you."

So, I got in her car and placed Ben on my lap.

Mom proceeded to tell me she had breast cancer. She told me she was going to need a double mastectomy. She said she had told Dad already. She told me she had noticed a lump a month ago, but knew that a lot of us were getting together for the first weekend of the NCAA Tournament in March (which we do every year), so she wanted to wait until after that to get it checked out. The news was not good.

Despite the weight of her information, Mom was very matter-of-fact about it. There was not a hint of despair, frustration, sadness or self-pity.

We sat in her car and talked about the situation, the course of action she was going to take and potential timelines. There wasn't a single tear shed or expletive uttered. That was Mom. She knew what the problem was, she knew what she was going to do about it and her attitude was "let's get on with it." I never saw Mom in a moment of self-pity about her cancer. Or anything else, for that matter. She would've surely seen that as a sign of weakness and she would've hated seeing self-pity in any of her children.

The Lesson: Life isn't meant to be fair. It doesn't matter what has happened to you that you feel is unjust or throws you off schedule. You need to assess the situation and take your next steps in the right direction, knowing you will continue to do your best. I must have heard Mom say "life isn't meant to be fair" a thousand times when I was a kid and complaining about something that didn't go my way.

In this case, regarding her cancer, Mom showed she truly understood what she had been teaching. She never asked "Why me?" Even mentioning that she never asked that question would've made her bristle, as it's so far away from her character. Another one of her sayings was "Complaining about it isn't going to help anything."

Mom was not about to waste time feeling sorry for herself or complaining about things she couldn't control. She was focused on doing what was necessary to get better.

———————————

Mom had a double-mastectomy in June 2005. I went with her to each of her appointments with her oncologists that spring and early that summer. My sister Katie, who is one year younger than me, came to Storm Lake the night before Mom's surgery, making the almost three-hour drive from her hometown of Cedar Falls, Iowa. After the surgery, Mom, Dad, Katie and I met with the surgeon, Dr. Matthews (not his real name), who explained how the surgery went and what they found.

Dr. Matthews explained that Mom's cancer was at stage four. This was not good news, as there isn't a stage five. Mom's tumor was large and it had metastasized to some lymph nodes. I remember that Mom listened to the surgeon detail this information and she nodded along as if she was listening to someone give her driving directions to the local baseball diamond. Her shoulders never slumped, her expression didn't drop and her voice didn't quiver. Mom just wanted the information and then wanted to do what was necessary to get better.

We talked with Mom about getting started very soon with chemotherapy. After those treatments, she would likely need radiation. The possible side effects were many and they were not pleasant. None of these developments seemed to throw Mom for a loop. She was ready to go to work to beat this thing.

I have no doubt that Mom's demeanor helped keep Dad settled and gave him at least a bit of peace. Possibly even some confidence. Her attitude had the same effect on me.

After the meeting with Dr. Matthews and our discussion about Mom's treatment plans, Katie stopped by my house on her way out of town. Katie is similar to Mom in many ways. Katie is smart, she has a strong faith, and she is direct. I asked her what she thought.

"That news today couldn't have been any worse," Katie said. She had a look on her face that said to me, "There is a good chance that Mom isn't going to survive this." But Katie didn't say that. And neither did I. We discussed the things the surgeon told us about the size of the tumor, the lymph nodes and the upcoming chemotherapy.

Katie and I were both very close to Mom. We knew Mom was going to be staring at a difficult physical battle and, at her age at the time (69), it was going to be even more daunting. Mom often said that, despite giving birth to eight children, the most difficult thing she ever had to do *physically* was quit smoking (which Mom and Dad did together on the same day in November of 1967).

Unfortunately, it appeared that quitting smoking was going to fall to number two on that list once Mom started chemotherapy.

Mom wasn't perfect. As wonderful as she was, she had her moments, like anyone else. Given the warped sense of humor of her eight children, we rarely let her forget any missteps, either.

When we were kids, one of our closest family friends was Leo Gallagher (no relation). He was my dad's age and although he was blind, Leo ran the local laundromat.

Our family took Leo to church each weekend, we had him over to our house for a meal or two each week and each of us kids took turns going to his apartment to read his mail, bills and newspapers to him. Leo was just like family. (In fact, Emily and I named our youngest child Leo mainly due to his influence on me.)

Leo was also an avid sports fan, so he would regularly go to our games with my parents. Dad would usually wander throughout the crowd and engage in various conversations, while Mom and Leo would sit together. Dad was usually much more vocal – and sometimes animated – at our games than Mom or Leo, so I think this arrangement was a benefit to all of them.

In the spring of 1994, the Storm Lake High School boys basketball team was playing a game for the right to advance to the Iowa State Tournament. My youngest brother Jerry was a senior starter on that team and I was the assistant coach. The game was played at our local college, Buena Vista, and the gym was packed with fans. I'm not sure you could've fit any more people in the bleachers.

The game was a classic, back-and-forth contest the entire way. Neither team led by more than four points. With each made basket, half of the crowd would go crazy. It was a madhouse.

As usual, Mom and Leo were sitting together, packed into the middle of the bleachers about three-quarters of the way up from the floor. Leo had his little radio with him as he always did, wearing headphones so he could listen to the play-by-play. Sometimes, Mom could tell him the details of the action, but not on this night. The gym was too loud.

The game went back and forth. One team would lead by a point and then the other team would lead by a point. With two minutes remaining in the game, Storm Lake made a basket to take a two-point lead and the crowd erupted. Mom jumped out of her seat, cheered and threw her arms into the air. However, when she raised her arms, she accidentally pulled the cord connecting Leo's headphones to his radio, which separated the two units and Leo's radio went straight down, between the bleachers, all the way crashing to the floor. So, in the biggest basketball game we had ever been directly associated with, there was Leo without his radio. Mom was extremely embarrassed.

The action continued and I think Mom tried to give Leo the play-by-play. Storm Lake won the game, 45-44, and advanced to the State Tournament in one of our most unforgettable sporting events as a family.

But Mom's exuberance and accidental destruction of Leo's radio was something we ribbed her about for the next 15 years. She always laughed right along, usually laughing harder than anyone else, as we would stretch the story into something much worse than what actually happened.

Mom always laughed easily. She had a loud, enthusiastic and distinctive laugh. In fact, there would be times she would start laughing so hard that I would imitate her, which would actually make her laugh even harder, until tears would roll down her cheeks.

The Lesson: You must be able to laugh at yourself. A sense of humor is so important and the ability to not take yourself too seriously is essential. Mom had an ego, no question about that, but she was always willing to take a joke and laugh right along. She was never defensive and very rarely poked fun at anyone else, but Mom was always willing to be the subject of the laughter. I think she loved to laugh as much as anyone I've ever known.

When I was in my 20s, I read some advice that you should record your parents' laughter. Thankfully, we did so in a video that my brother Jerry and I made in 2001, depicting Dad as one of the "Greatest Athletes of the Century" (an obvious mockumentary). We interviewed Mom for a segment in that video and at one point, she threw her head back and laughed out loud. I love seeing that part of the video and hearing her laughter. Without a doubt, Mom's laugh is one of my all-time favorite sounds.

CHAPTER 2

TUESDAY, DECEMBER 30, 2008

This morning, my sister Katie drives to Storm Lake from her home in Cedar Falls, approximately 150 miles away. Dad, Katie and I spend most of the day at the hospital with Mom. We rotate in and out of Mom's room, so there is always one (but usually two) of us there with her.

Mom's pain is greater than I expected it to be. She is a very tough person with an extremely high pain tolerance, but she is clearly very uncomfortable.

Even though I have seen Mom almost every day for the last few weeks, I am surprised at how old and frail she looks in that hospital bed. Her skin has lost much of its color, her eyes look sunken and it appears her face has aged 15 years since I saw her this weekend. It is shocking, but her spirit is still good.

I leave the hospital over the noon hour to catch up on some work in my office at home. My house is two blocks from the hospital, so it's easy for me to go back and forth in a few minutes. When I call Dad early this afternoon, he tells me that Mom is still a little tired and shaky, but that she feels better. "She ate more for lunch today than she has in a week and a half," Dad says. "So, that's good." I agree with Dad that this is a good sign, although I wonder if we are each trying to convince *ourselves* as much as we are trying to convince each other.

Later this afternoon, around 2 p.m., my 35-year-old brother Ed arrives at the hospital. He made the 85-mile drive south from his home in Jackson, Minnesota. When Ed walks into Mom's hospital room, the first thing Mom says when she sees him is, "Oh shit."

Dad, Katie and I get a big laugh out of that. Ed plays it up pretty well with a shoulder shrug and a line about this being the reaction he typically gets when he enters a room.

Mom laughs too, but her reaction is based on not wanting people to make a fuss over her. She is a very strong person and she doesn't want anyone to feel sorry for her. I think she saw Ed and immediately felt some guilt or disappointment that she had caused him to feel he needed to drive to Storm Lake today.

I think she was already feeling a little guilty that Katie and I were spending the day with her. When she saw Ed, maybe it was the pain meds causing her to let her guard down (she rarely swore), but it was a sincere reaction.

Ed spends much of the afternoon sitting right beside Mom's bed. Dad, Katie, Ed, Mom and I visit about various things, from the winter weather to the football season. We share plenty of laughs. Ed is the type of guy who *everyone* likes. He's a big guy, he's smart, he can be a man of few words, and he's got a wonderful sense of humor. He's also very low key and stays on an even keel, rarely showing any emotion, good or bad.

So, it surprises me when, around 5 p.m., Ed leans over to Mom to say good-bye and his voice cracks. He tells her "I love you" and he bends down and kisses her on the forehead.

I think it surprises Mom, too.

We've never been a family that shows a lot of emotion. We've also never been a family that says "I love you" to each other very much. And if anyone was going to do either of those things, Ed wouldn't be my first guess.

When I walk with Ed out to his vehicle in the snowy, wet parking lot, he turns to me and says, "I was shocked at how bad she looked. I didn't know what to expect, but this is *bad*."

Ed is right, as usual.

A little later, after Mom has eaten some supper, they start her on a morphine drip for her pain. At around 7 p.m., the nurse tells Dad, Katie and I that Mom would be asleep pretty quickly as the morphine takes effect.

Dad, Katie and I told Mom "good night" and we walk across the hall and down one room to a little waiting room that has a TV, kitchen area, a table and some chairs. We know that Mom's doctor, Dr. Williams (not his real name), would be making a trip up to check on Mom in a little bit and we want to visit with him.

When the three of us step into the waiting room, there is no more time for small talk about the weather or the football season. There is no more laughter. The mood shifts immediately. We had all put on our best front for Mom today, but we all know today has not gone anywhere near as well as we had hoped.

"I think she knew," Dad says, fighting back tears. "I think she knew this was her last Christmas." Katie leans over and hugs Dad. I think the last time that I saw my dad cry was when his brother Daryl died in 1979. I was nine years old at that time, so it has been 30 years.

Dad, Katie and I all feel the same thing, but we held out hope for good news from Dr. Williams, who arrives a few minutes later to visit with us.

Dr. Williams is a soft-spoken, sensitive man, who has been Mom's doctor for most of the past two decades. We are seated in four chairs in the waiting room, with Katie sitting directly across from the doctor. This is good, because Katie has all the right initial questions and all of the pertinent follow-up questions ready to go. I'm not sure if it's Katie's background in social work, her experience as a hospice worker, or her mix of intelligence and quick thinking, but I am impressed by her ability to keep asking the doctor insightful questions about Mom's condition, what Mom's various numbers should be tomorrow and the next day, and what we should expect. Dad and I have our questions too, but Katie is clearly leading the discussion.

The doctor remains calm and measured with his responses, sitting cross-legged on his chair and speaking in a soothing, unwavering tone of voice. But he is also nervously picking at little imaginary pieces of lint on his pant legs, so he isn't totally comfortable, either with the questions or with what he is able to say. I'm sure he isn't usually cross-examined like this by family members, but Katie has a smooth way of asking direct questions without making a person feel "on the spot."

Dr. Williams does his best to answer the questions without saying, "I think Anne's cancer has returned." He talks about possibilities of complications from combinations of medications she has been taking, the possibility of Mom's gall bladder being the issue, Mom's platelet, white blood cell and bilirubin counts, as well as the new antibiotic they started her on today. He says it's a good sign her appetite was much better today. He says there were some spots on Mom's spine they could see on the MRI, and there were also some spots on her liver. But he says these could be nothing at all, they don't know at this point.

Our conversation with the doctor lasts 30 minutes. He says he will come through to check on Mom in the morning between 7:30 and 8 a.m., and they will do the ultrasound on Mom's gall bladder in the morning, as well.

After Dr. Williams leaves, Dad, Katie and I visit in the waiting room for another five minutes. We know today has been rough, but we also feel some optimism due to Mom's appetite and the hope tomorrow might bring progress. Katie is going to stay at the hospital with Mom tonight, but we all stop in to see Mom just for a minute, even though she has likely been sound asleep for a half-hour.

But she's not asleep.

Despite the exhaustion she must have been feeling and the morphine going through her system for almost an hour, Mom is wide awake.

I'm amazed. How could she stay awake?

"So, what did he say?" Mom asks.

Mom has managed to stay awake for the last hour on sheer will and determination to learn the details of our conversation with Dr. Williams. She wants the information, she wants to know the facts, she doesn't want anything "sugar coated" for her. And she is one strong-willed woman.

The Lesson: Get the facts and do the research, because information is power. I think Mom's ability to stay awake through her exhaustion – and despite her medication – was the most impressive thing I witnessed on this day. Katie's ability to rattle off question after follow-up question to the doctor was a close second, and it was a skill she surely learned from Mom. In each of these instances, the goal was to get more information, dig a little deeper to arrive at more facts, because this effort will help determine what needs to happen next.

———————

Mom was a wonderful teacher, who loved to encourage and challenge her students. She had a way of motivating a child (whether one of her own children or a student in the classroom) to stretch a little farther than the child was used to and get that individual to see his or her true potential.

I remember when I was in second grade, I used to give my teacher fits. I was always talking, laughing or stirring up trouble of some sort, and being a general distraction during class. One day, I found myself sitting on a chair in the hallway with masking tape all over the lower half of my face, covering my mouth. The tape had been stuck there by my teacher. That was a pretty good sign, even to a second-grader, that I was probably talking too much when I was supposed to be quiet.

My second-grade teacher asked Mom at a conference what she should do with me. I think the teacher thought I might be a discipline problem, but Mom felt I was probably bored in class and needed more to do. Something that would challenge me a little bit more. Mom told the teacher to "give him a topic to research and write a report about, and he will enjoy that."

Sure enough, my second-grade teacher gave me some individual projects like that and I was happy. I'm sure my behavior improved in the classroom, too. I remember researching in our encyclopedias at home and writing reports about subjects like dinosaurs, President John Kennedy and the solar system.

Mom had taught me how to research information and write reports, and she also taught my teacher about challenging a student to stretch a little bit. Everyone learned something. And everyone benefited.

The Lesson: Challenge yourself. Another one of my mother's favorite sayings was, "Intelligent people don't get bored." Mom felt there was always a world of information available to you, so there was always something to research and learn. She also felt that, if you didn't feel like reading, you could always grab a sheet of paper and a pencil, and write a story, or draw a picture using your own imagination.

Mom harped on that point consistently when we were growing up. Push yourself to learn more, to do more and to become more. Don't fall into the trap of going down the easy road or just doing enough to get by. Mom was determined to make sure her children, and her students, squeezed the most they could out of their potential.

One night in 1980, when I was 11 years old, Mom and my oldest sibling Maggie (18 years old at the time) were in an argument in the kitchen. Maggie had made some questionable decisions and Mom was explaining to Maggie how she should improve in some areas and begin to take responsibility for some things. It's probably a pretty common discussion/argument for a parent to have with an 18-year-old child, who saw herself as an 18-year-old *adult*.

I listened to this argument with two of my older brothers, Dan (16 at the time) and Tim (12). We were in a bedroom about 10 feet from the kitchen and we had the door closed. We remained quiet, partly so we could hear every word and partly so that we wouldn't be discovered.

With each verbal jab that was made by Mom and Maggie, we winced or made faces to each other, showing how powerful we thought the comment had been. It was like being at a sporting event, except that Dan, Tim and I could only communicate with facial expressions and fist pumps.

At the peak of the discussion, Maggie made a comment that Mom was treating her differently than the "other kids" and that somehow, Maggie was getting the short end of the stick. She accused Mom of thinking that she was "not as good" as the other kids. Mom responded immediately … and as she did with all of her comments, remained calm and direct.

"Maggie, that's not true," Mom said. "I have EIGHT children and only ONE of them marches to the beat of a different drummer…"

I remember Dan, Tim and I looking at each other with great anticipation as we were absolutely certain that Mom was going to name Maggie as that lone, odd duck of the group. We felt this would be the knockout punch in this discussion and we braced ourselves as Mom completed her thought.

"… And that's *Marty*," she said.

I felt my heart drop. My facial expression changed immediately from excited anticipation to mouth-hanging-open stunned. Dan and Tim looked at me like I had an extra arm growing out of my forehead … and they tried to stifle their laughter as they pointed at me in delight. It was doubly difficult for them to do that, because we were trying to be so quiet. But I don't remember another word of the discussion Mom and Maggie had that night.

"Why do I march to the beat of a different drummer?" I asked myself. Why does Mom think that *I'm* the odd duck? How could Mom single me out like that to my sister? It felt like such an insult and it also felt a little like I had been betrayed.

So, what did I do? I did the same thing that any other kid, who had seen each episode of "The Brady Bunch" several times, would do. I pouted. I pouted up a storm around Mom the next couple of days. Normally, Mom would not respond to such childish and selfish behavior. But she had no idea I had heard her "different drummer" comment, so I think she was actually curious.

Mom waited until we were the only two people in the basement living room. She asked me what was wrong.

I told her I heard her "different drummer" comment, that it hurt my feelings and I didn't want to be *different*.

Mom listened to me (as she always did), then looked a bit relieved and explained what she had meant to her 11-year-old son. Mom told me that, in her eyes, "marching to the beat of a different drummer" was a compliment and that doing things your own way is a good thing. She explained to me that it's not only OK to be different, but being unique is a positive trait and something to be proud of. By the time Mom was done talking, I was feeling full of self-esteem. I thought Mom saw something in me that nobody else could see. I was pumped.

Ever since that day, I have wanted to be a little different from my siblings and my peers. I have embraced looking at things in a different way sometimes. And I have tried to live my life in a unique way … and realize that it's OK – a good thing, really – to go my own way, rather than to follow along with what everybody else does all the time.

I have Mom to thank for that. To this day, I think about that "drummer" comment at least once per week. It might have been a throw-away comment in an argument that Mom and Maggie had back in 1980, but through Mom's conversation with me a few days later, it became one of the most important compliments I've ever received.

The Lesson: Be true to yourself. There is no doubt each person has special qualities that make him or her unique. Mom wanted me to understand it's important to let these character-istics shine through and to be myself, even if that might mean I would be a little different from other kids my age. That's not only OK, she told me, but that's something to be proud of. To me, she was telling me to be myself and to avoid always following along with the crowd.

CHAPTER 3

WEDNESDAY, DECEMBER 31, 2008

I arrive at Mom's hospital room shortly before 7:30 a.m. Katie spent the night there and Dad has just arrived, as well. When I walk in the room, Mom is in a wheelchair as she has just been in the bathroom. As weak as she was yesterday, she appears even worse this morning. It is all Mom can do to muster the strength (with two people helping) to get out of that wheelchair and back into her bed.

Dr. Williams arrives shortly before 8 a.m. and visits with Mom for a bit. Then, Katie and I stop him in the hallway to get any further thoughts he might have.

The doctor tells us that Mom's white blood cell count is down to 14,700 from 16,000 yesterday, so that is going in the right direction, and it shows that Mom's body is fighting off the infection. However, he is concerned about her platelets, which have dropped from 80,000 yesterday to 64,000 today. He says that with her platelets that low, they would likely not perform surgery on Mom's gall bladder, so they need to get those numbers to increase. I think he told us last night that if the platelet count falls to 40,000 or 50,000, they start thinking about a transfusion.

The doctor also tells us he is concerned Mom's lungs are collapsing a bit as she has not been getting any exercise for a while and so Dr. Williams wants Mom to get up and walk around some today. After watching Mom struggle (even with the aid of two people) to get from her wheelchair to her bed this morning, Katie and I figure it will take an act of God for Mom to "walk around some" anytime soon.

But Mom proves to be even tougher than we thought. Plus, she receives an unexpected boost today when my brother Tim drops in for a visit shortly after lunch.

For the last two decades, we have teased Mom that Tim is her "favorite." We take situations and blow them out of proportion to help make our case, and Mom just laughs. But there is at least *some* truth to it. Mom does have a special place in her heart for Tim. (On a related note perhaps, Tim is EASILY her son who is most similar to Dad.)

I stay in Mom's room today for the rest of the morning. Dad, Katie and I visit with each other, and with Mom, when she's awake. Mom has an appetite and eats a little lunch over the noon hour. At about 2 p.m., she decides to take a shower, so I leave to get caught up on some work in my office at home.

Tim arrives shortly after that, making the one-hour drive from his home in Moville, Iowa.

I pick my two children up from school at about 3:20 p.m. Molly is in second grade and Ben is in kindergarten. They are attending West Elementary School in Storm Lake, which is the same school Mom attended during her elementary years. I bring the kids home and I work a little bit more. Then, at about 5 p.m., the kids and I head to Wal-Mart to get some necessities.

On my way to Wal-Mart, I call Tim to get an update on Mom's condition. Tim seems to think Mom is doing great. He says she was up and walking around this afternoon. "What?" I ask. "What do you *mean*?" I am shocked, given her condition yesterday and this morning.

Tim reiterates that Mom was up and walking around. I insist on specifics. He tells me that Mom walked from the shower down the hall to her room. I ask, "You mean that she had people holding onto her and she took a few steps?"

Tim tells me again, "No … she walked down the hall. I was there and saw her do it." I know Tim must wonder why I'm so incredulous. He had not seen Mom yesterday or this morning. I wonder if after she had eaten some lunch today, maybe she gained a little energy. Plus, I'm sure that she was very happy to see Tim. (I highly doubt he received an "oh shit" reaction.)

But still. I found the "up and walking around" information hard to believe.

Molly, Ben and I arrive at Wal-Mart and as we walk through the front door, we run into Juli Kwikkel, a friend of Mom's. Juli is the elementary school principal, so she and Mom had a lot of conversations in the last several years about the field of education. They also went on a few trips throughout the country to different conferences together. Juli knows my mom well, but she hasn't seen her in a few weeks.

After we exchanged hellos, Juli looks a little concerned and asks, "How's your mom doing? I haven't seen her in a while."

For some reason, I figured Juli knew that Mom is in the hospital. I guess it's that part of you that, when you're experiencing something so large in your life, you almost assume everyone else knows it's happening. But they don't. People have their own lives and their own issues to deal with. Juli has no idea about Mom.

I lower my voice so Molly and Ben can't hear. "Not good, Juli," I tell her. "She's actually in the hospital right now. We're going right back to see her after we get a few things here."

"Oh," Juli says. "Is it her *back*? I know that was really bothering her before Christmas."

"No," I reply. "I think it's much more serious than that. She's in pretty tough shape."

I don't think I used the word "cancer," but Juli knows from my tone of voice what I mean. "Can I see her?" she asks. "What's her room number?" I give Juli the room number and tell her Mom would be happy to see her.

I know Mom would enjoy seeing Juli and visiting with her. It was purely by chance I ran into Juli while heading into Wal-Mart, but maybe some divine intervention had something to do with it. Maybe that was one of the little blessings that Mom received for saying those thousands upon thousands of rosaries in her life. I don't know. But I do know this: I don't go to Wal-Mart all that often and I've never seen Juli Kwikkel there before that day or since.

After we got our shopping done, the kids and I head straight to the hospital. Tim had left a little earlier as he needed to get back home to his family. Dad, Katie, Molly, Ben and I sit in Mom's room, along with Juli, and we all enjoy a fun conversation with Mom that evening. We share stories and lots of laughs. I know Mom was touched that Juli stopped by to see her.

Today is New Year's Eve and there are some "party hats" in Mom's room, so she has Molly and Ben each try one on and take one home. The kids have fun with that, and they also enjoy watching Grandma blow into a little device that measures the power in her lungs. Mom makes it a fun visit for the kids, which is very typical of her, always putting someone else first and especially being cognizant of how a trip to the hospital might otherwise seem scary and uncomfortable to a couple of young children.

After Juli heads for home, the nurse wants Mom to get up and walk up and down the hall one more time today. So, Dad, Katie, the kids and I go out in the hall to cheer her on. Katie tells me that Mom has actually made it up and down the hall THREE TIMES already today. I still find it hard to believe until I see Mom walking with my own eyes.

Mom isn't moving quickly, but she *is* walking on her own. She is smiling as she talks to Molly and Ben on her way down the hall. There is a Christmas tree at the end of the hall and when Mom makes it that far, she gives a "high five" to both Molly and Ben. Then, Mom turns around and walks all the way back to her room. I am amazed. It's an incredible turn-around from what I saw this morning, when Mom could barely get out of the wheelchair and into her bed.

After her walk, Mom is exhausted. Katie and I decide to take Molly and Ben out for supper, to their favorite place in town, The Villager. Dad is going to stay with Mom while we are gone and then I will drop Katie off to stay in Mom's room for the night again tonight.

While we are eating supper with my kids, Katie and I discuss how we are definitely encouraged by what we saw today. Mom's lungs HAD to be doing better now than they were this morning. And we feel her pain level is better than it had been yesterday. We are hopeful that Mom's appetite will gradually increase, and that she might continue to walk around and get some more exercise tomorrow. Everything seems to be on the upswing.

Katie and I talk about what a difference that 24 hours made. When Ed left Storm Lake yesterday, he might have been wondering if Mom would live through the night. When Tim left Storm Lake today, he might have been wondering if Mom would be discharged from the hospital tomorrow.

At the end of the day, we all have a renewed hope that Mom is going to be OK and that our worst fears will not be realized.

The Lesson: Keep fighting. One thing Mom didn't have much sympathy for was whining. She always placed the importance on looking ahead and making the best out of your situation. Mom was constantly reinforcing the idea to avoid excuses and to keep working hard, keep forging ahead. She made the point numerous times about focusing on what you can control and then doing the very best you can do.

Through all of the games she watched me play as a boy, the only times she ever got upset with me were when I would complain to an umpire or referee. Mom had no time for that. She wanted me to accept the decision and keep fighting, keep working hard and keep looking forward. Mom continued to do that throughout her battle with cancer.

———————

Adding Juli to the mix that night was not unusual. Mom was always happy to see additional friends and family, and enjoy the conversations that would ensue. She was always fine with us bringing home a friend after school, allowing them to stay for supper and spend all kinds of time at our house.

People like John Nus, Ky Betts and Chad Triplett spent enough time with our family they practically *became* part of the family during their high school years. I know that more than once, Mom or Dad would come home in the late afternoon and nobody would be at our house ... except Ky Betts, who would be sitting at the kitchen table, eating a bowl of cereal. Now, THAT is high a level of comfort.

The Lesson: Be welcoming. Prior to Ed's senior year of high school in the summer of 1991, Mom and Dad welcomed a foreign exchange student into their household. Erik Eldhagen, of Stockholm, Sweden, came to Storm Lake in July and would stay for one year.

At the time, I remember thinking it was a bit of a gamble by Mom and Dad. What if this kid was a troublemaker? Or had nothing in common with Ed and Jerry, who were still in high school at the time?

But, all fears were erased the first night we sat down for dinner. Erik was engaging, brilliant, funny and a tremendous amount of fun to be around. Throughout that year from July 1991 through July 1992, Erik became a wonderful part of our family. We all loved him.

Early on, he stayed out a bit too late, but Mom corrected that pretty quickly. She was more patient with the dozens of tiny bottles of Tabasco sauce he had throughout the kitchen. But the bottom line was that anytime Erik was around, there were great conversations and much laughter. His intelligence kept us on our toes and his stories kept us entertained.

I'm sure Erik was participating in the exchange program in order to learn something from his experience. Ultimately, though, it was the Gallaghers who gained so much from adding Erik to our family.

Two years later, Erik came back to Storm Lake for the summer of 1994. He stayed at my parents' house again … and it was fantastic to have that time together. He returned to Storm Lake with his wife Susie and son Alexander in November 2007. Mom and Dad were thrilled to see Erik, reconnect with him as an adult … and they were extremely impressed with Susie.

Erik has returned to Storm Lake multiple times since then and it is always terrific to see him, catch up and share stories.

Looking back, I think it showed how Mom and Dad felt it was important to be welcoming and provide a warm, friendly atmosphere at our house. As a result, I think our friends – and our brother Erik from Sweden – always felt comfortable and welcome.

When Mom passed away, Erik sent a $1,000 memorial check to Dad, earmarked for a scholarship created in her name. "This gift is merely symbolic in relation to all I have received at your house," Erik wrote in a letter to Dad. "So glad I got to see Anne again and introduce my family. Felt so warmly welcomed – like coming back home in fact. Very few things matter more than that feeling."

———————

Mom was a very kind and gracious person, but she also enjoyed competing. Whether she was playing a card game, Trivial Pursuit,

Boggle, Uno or something else, she competed to win. She was also among the loudest fans at our sporting events – always in a positive manner and always enthusiastic.

One thing she repeatedly told us when we played basketball might surprise some people, even those who knew her pretty well. "If you're going to foul him, foul him *good*," she would say. "Do not let him make the basket." That might sound a little harsh, but her point was if you couldn't stop an opponent from scoring with your foul, then don't foul him at all. Otherwise, she saw it as a half-hearted effort.

The Lesson: Compete hard. Two of Mom's all-time favorite athletes were Pete Rose and Derek Jeter. Both guys won a lot of games, for sure, but what she really liked about them was they both played hard all the time. In Mom's opinion, if you're going to do something, do it *right*. And if there is a scoreboard, then play to *win*.

———————

Seeing Mom's energy level make such a positive turn today reminds me of one of the unique things that Mom used to do when we were kids.

She made sugar sandwiches.

That's right. Sugar sandwiches. It's not a complicated recipe. You take a piece of bread, spread butter on one side, pour sugar on the butter, then fold the bread over to keep the butter and sugar on the inside. That's a sugar sandwich.

Sugar sandwiches were crunchy, sweet, and obviously, full of sugar, so when you ate a few of those as a 10-year-old kid, your energy level was going to shoot up. Mom would make a plateful of sugar sandwiches when we got home from school, we would eat those sandwiches and Mom would tell us to go outside and play. We would go out to our large yard and play ball for a couple of hours, burning off that energy in a positive way.

Plus, by getting her six sons outside (I'm not sure if Maggie or Katie ever needed to eat the sugar sandwiches), Mom would have a certain amount of peace and quiet to continue her never-ending work on the laundry and time to make supper for the family. Meanwhile, the six Gallagher boys would play baseball, basketball or football outside until we heard "the bell."

What's "the bell?"

When it was time for a meal, Mom had an old cowbell that would signal to us kids that it was time to go inside to eat. Mom would open the back door and clang that bell five or six times – good and loud – with a clear purpose. Clang! Clang! CLANG! Clang! Clang! CLANG! At that time, our friends would get on their bikes and head for home … and the Gallagher kids would head inside to eat a meal.

Sugar sandwiches and a cowbell. One meant it was time to go outside and the other meant it was time to come in. Simple stuff, but very effective.

The Lesson: Keep it simple. There wasn't a lot of complicated "read-between-the-lines" kind of stuff with Mom. She said what she meant and meant what she said. When she didn't want a bunch of kids underfoot because she was trying to get something done, she would make sugar sandwiches and tell us to go outside and play.

When she had supper ready and wanted the neighborhood kids to go home and the Gallagher kids to come inside to eat, she would ring a cowbell. Everyone understood those things. Nobody challenged any of it. It was a win-win scenario for all who were involved. It made sense. And it worked.

Another lesson she was teaching is that it's good for kids to get outside and play. It's good for them physically, and it's good for them mentally and socially. It's good for kids to make up rules to games together and learn how to settle disputes on their own. It's good for kids to learn how to win and lose, and get along with others. Growing up in our house on Prairie Avenue in Strawberry Point, we didn't spend any time playing video games. Not as long as there was bread, butter and sugar in the house ... and a big yard outside.

Mom's parents, Everett and Cyrilla Stock, lived in Storm Lake. Everett was a banker and excellent with numbers. He spoke quietly, dressed impeccably, smoked a pipe and had a terrific sense of humor. Cyrilla earned her teaching degree from the University of Iowa in the early 1920s. She was smart, tough, direct and a disciplinarian with very little time for nonsense.

Dad's mother, Helen, also earned her teaching degree. She attended Grinnell College and taught country school until she married Eugene Gallagher in 1917. It is a rare thing to have TWO grandmothers of that generation who earned college degrees. But it shows the value of education in our family.

My parents met on a blind date set up by a mutual friend named Bill Barron. "We went to a St. Patrick's Day Dance in Cedar Rapids," Dad says. "And so that started the romance."

Dad was 36 and Mom was 25 when they started dating in March 1961. Shortly thereafter, Dad drove to Storm Lake to meet Everett and Cyrilla. He likes to tell the story about letting Cyrilla know he was serious about her daughter. "I told Cyrilla when she was working in the kitchen that I thought a lot of Anne and we might get married sometime," Dad says with a smile. "And Cyrilla said, 'I've got to get this roast in the oven.' She ignored me." Dad always laughs when he delivers that line.

Forty years later, Jerry and I created the mockumentary of Dad featured as one of the "Greatest Athletes of the Century." It was a ridiculous video that still generates laughs for our family today. At one point, we interviewed Mom and asked her what drew her to Dad initially. "He didn't care if I drank or smoked," she said, tilting her head back with a big laugh.

Fewer than five months after their first date, Mom and Dad were married on August 5, 1961.

The Lesson: Education is important ... and so is a sense of humor.

CHAPTER 4

THURSDAY, JANUARY 1, 2009

It's the first day of a new year, 2009. The air is crisp and the temperature is in the low 20s this morning. New Year's Day is a time for hope and optimism, which is what I'm feeling as I drive to the hospital shortly after 7 a.m. Katie spent the night with Mom, so she's there when I arrive at Mom's room on the second floor. Dad is there too. After last night, I feel hopeful that Mom's numbers are improving and perhaps she is turning a corner.

A few minutes after I arrive, Dr. Williams comes to see Mom and gives us a report that lets some air out of my optimism balloon. And Mom appears to be exhausted.

After meeting with the doctor and visiting with Katie and Dad for a while, I head back home. Because I'm the only sibling who lives in the same town as our parents, I have become the communications director for our family. I send email updates to the rest of the family to keep them posted on any news regarding Mom and Dad. At 9:24 a.m., I send the following email to my seven siblings:

When I dropped Katie back off at the hospital last night, she said that Mom was already asleep for the night, which was good. That was about 8:30 p.m. Katie said that Mom slept pretty well until about 4 a.m. when the nurses got her up because she was bleeding quite a bit from her IV spot. They had to poke her six or seven times to get back into her veins, but Katie said that Mom slept through most of that.

Dr. Williams came in to see her at about 7:15 this morning and his report wasn't all that encouraging. Here is what he had to say:

- The platelet numbers haven't changed since yesterday (in his words, they are 'stable').

- Mom's liver function is slightly down, but that could be a natural variation.

- He is ordering another CT scan of the gall bladder and liver. We are not sure if this will take place today or tomorrow. And he's going to request that they take a good look at the lower spine with that scan, as well.

- Depending on what the platelets do the next couple of days, Dr. Williams may want to do a bone marrow biopsy.

- Another option with the platelets is a platelets transfusion, but Dr. Williams said that's a *short-term remedy that would only help for a few days. That decision would ultimately be up to Dr. Williams, Mom and Dad.*

- *There is no change in Mom's lung function from yesterday to today, which Dr. Williams was hoping there would be. He's adding another treatment four times per day in addition to what she was doing yesterday for her lungs. If that doesn't improve her lungs by tomorrow, he'll order a chest x-ray tomorrow because he does not want her to get pneumonia.*

After Dr. Williams left, the nurses got Mom up at about 7:45 a.m. to go to the bathroom. Then, she sat up to eat breakfast and ate a little bit. She had a heating pad on her back. And she fell right back to sleep.

All of this stuff this morning was discouraging, considering the incredible progress that seemed to be made yesterday afternoon/evening. However, Dad was quick to point out that Mom is definitely not a morning person, so maybe she'll bounce back this afternoon again, just like she did yesterday. Let's hope for that and that the platelet numbers and lung function start to show signs of improvement by tomorrow.

I will keep you posted. Feel free to call my cell or Katie's cell if you have questions.

After sending that email, I drive back to the hospital. Katie and I meet in the hallway to visit about Mom's condition. We are both concerned that her cancer has returned and this is why her numbers are not bouncing back. We feel Dr. Williams is telling us all he can, but we wish we *knew* the reason for Mom failing so rapidly … and then, of course, what – if anything – can be done to help her.

While Katie and I are visiting, another doctor – Dr. Davis (not his real name) – walks by. We've known each other for several years and like me, he's a big fan of the Iowa Hawkeyes. When he says hello, he asks what we're doing here. It's New Year's Day, after all, and the Hawkeye football team is playing in the Outback Bowl this morning. I explain to him what's going on with Mom and ask him if there's any way to know if her cancer has returned and spread.

Dr. Davis asks me to follow him. He goes into a room where he sits down and logs into a computer. He checks into her file and looks at her scans. Dr. Davis sighs, points to the image of Mom's liver and says, "You see this area here?" as he points to a vast majority of her liver image. "This looks like cancer to me." He says he can't say for sure without more information, but his expression and tone make it clear he is confident. He apologizes for the bad news, shakes my hand and I thank him. Dr. Davis tightens his lips, nods and walks away.

Katie and I look at each other. We are crushed by the news, but also somewhat relieved to feel like we know something now.

If Mom's cancer has now spread to her liver, her condition makes sense, but her chances of fighting it are not good. She has barely been awake so far today and, in fact, she would open her eyes for less than an hour total as the day goes along. Pain management has become the key phrase, it seems.

"I should call the others and let them know," I say.

"Right," Katie says. "People should probably come and see her right away, if they can get here."

We both feel Mom may not have much time left. I tell Katie I'll go home and make the calls, while she can go back and stay with Mom and Dad in Mom's room.

I drive back home and start making calls. One after another, I deliver the news and ask my siblings to come back to Storm Lake to see Mom. Maggie and her husband Al will make the drive from Radcliffe, Iowa; Dan says he'll come from his home in Waukee, Iowa; Joe will fly from St. Louis to Omaha, then drive here; Tim will be on his way here shortly; Ed will be get here as soon as he can; Jerry will drive six hours from Eau Claire, Wisconsin this afternoon.

Everyone was here two weeks ago to celebrate Christmas as a family. Now, without hesitation, everyone is coming back.

The Lesson: Be there for each other. Mom always made it clear with her actions that being there for someone you love is extremely important. Not only did she refuse to miss any of our ballgames, performances or concerts when we were kids, she was also always willing to have conversations about any successes or failures we had as adults. Nobody was more supportive than Mom ... and nobody enjoyed spending time with their kids and grandkids more than she did.

Getting news or hearing information you don't like or want is part of life. Mom would say that you have to deal with it.

Throughout our lives, Mom has always been very supportive with her children, but also honest and, when necessary, critical. As a result, I think each of us improved at accepting advice and understanding we don't always have the answers.

Jerry had the lead role in the Storm Lake High School musical (or play) all four years he was a high school student. His sophomore year, he was the lead in the play "Snoopy" and as teenagers often do, Jerry decided to push the envelope a bit. One of his lines was supposed to be, "Sorry Charlie, you're out of luck."

Instead, Jerry said, "Sorry Charlie, you're *screwed*!"

As a 15-year old, Jerry thought this was funny. And it was the last performance of the play, which sometimes leads students to make different choices.

Mom was not amused.

She pulled Jerry aside immediately after he got home. "She gave me a tongue lashing," Jerry said. "She wanted me to apologize to the play director and the cast. 'Don't you know what that word *means*?'

"Her point was to apologize when you make a mistake. Own it. That's something I've tried to instill in my own kids."

Six or seven years later, Jerry was the news anchor at our local ABC-TV affiliate in Sioux City. Mom and Dad watched every broadcast and videotaped the ones they couldn't see live. It was not uncommon for Mom to let Jerry know when he mispronounced a word ... or share her opinion on his jacket, shirt and tie choices.

"While she wasn't comfortable being center stage, Mom knew the importance of communication in front of large groups," Jerry said. "She felt that EVERY WORD mattered. She was my first editor as a writer and my biggest critic as a broadcaster. She instilled the value of creative expression and accuracy. I'm so grateful for that."

The Lesson: "Because I said so." Sometimes, we didn't want to hear the criticism ... or we didn't like the answer to a question. Or maybe we just didn't like the explanation provided. But we needed to listen and try to learn from this feedback just as intently as we accepted any praise.

In the spring of 1987, when I was a senior at Starmont High School, I was the emcee at our high school "pops concert," a talent show of sorts, featuring various band and choir groups, that lasted a couple of hours. There was a show on Friday night, followed by the same show on Saturday night.

I felt confident with my role, so I didn't practice or prepare much for this event.

But then, about halfway through Friday night's performance, the choir was finishing a song when the band director rushed up to me and said, "One of the girls in the choir needs to change her outfit before the next act, so you're going to need to go out there and kill five minutes."

I smirked. But he was serious.

I had nothing prepared for this. Nor was I aware it could be a possibility.

So, I went on stage, explained the situation, told a couple of jokes and ended up getting the crowd to sing "Row Row Row Your Boat" in the round. It killed five minutes. When the next act was ready, I introduced them and went backstage. The band director was happy. I was happy.

After the show that night, I fully expected Mom and Dad to tell me what a fantastic job I had done as the emcee. Most of the other parents expressed something similar to me. But Mom had no praise to share. *None.* She saw that I was not prepared for the time I had to kill and thought it came off as a half-hearted effort. So that night, I went to the local gas station and rented a standup comedy videotape.

The Lesson: Be prepared. The performance on Saturday night ran much more smoothly. I filled the five-minute gap with a couple of stories and a few of Howie Mandel's most appropriate comedy bits. Everyone was pleased, from the director to my parents ... to me.

When I was coaching the boys' basketball team at Storm Lake High School in the 1990s, one of my favorite things was coming home after a Friday night home game and seeing my parents' car at my house. Mom and Dad enjoyed coming over to rehash the game, but also to share in the postgame fun after a victory … or to show support after a disappointing loss.

If I was ever having difficulty motivating a boy or getting through to him, Mom was an outstanding resource for me, given her decades of experience in the classroom (and as a parent). She was always interested in conversations about teaching, coaching, wins and losses … and how to learn something about each experience.

Mom was also a phenomenal resource for me when I was a single parent, raising two young children. When Molly and Ben were young, Mom was always there as a sounding board for me … and no question or scenario seemed too big or small to talk to her about. She would often read books, play games and tell stories with my kids. Mom would ride along and help with my kids whether we were going to one of their cousin's basketball games in Moville or to a Wiggles concert in Council Bluffs. She was always there and she appeared to love every minute of it.

Before her last Christmas, Mom took Molly and Ben uptown in Storm Lake one afternoon. I can't remember the reason she gave me. But she took the kids to "Santa's Secret Workshop," where kids could shop on their own for a few low-priced gifts and get them gift-wrapped. Molly and Ben were so happy to surprise me with a gift under the tree. It was a black-and-gold Hawkeye cup with two pencils, a candy cane and some M&Ms inside. Without question, it was the best gift I received. Mom knew what something like that would mean to me and she never failed to come through. That cup remained on my office desk for several years.

Mom was also a night owl. She would stay up well past midnight regularly. When we were kids, she would spend that time doing laundry and mending clothes. After her children had grown, she would spend those late-night hours reading. After she retired in 2001, she could sleep in until 9 or 10 a.m. (or beyond), so she would stay up even later. One of her favorite things to do was stay up and engage in late-night conversations with her children when they were in town. I tend to stay up late too, so this was also in my wheelhouse.

If Katie, Joe and Jerry were in town, for example, we would all stay up late with Mom asking questions, telling stories and getting advice from her. We all thoroughly enjoyed the discussions, which were filled with a mixture of laughter and awe as she would share her stories from the 1960s and 1970s about raising a house full of children.

Eventually, someone would look at the clock, realize it was 2 a.m. and start the process of winding down the conversation. But Mom would always be the last to call it a day. If someone wanted to talk some more or ask one more question, she would happily oblige.

She was an amazing mother to all of us when my siblings and I were young, but I think she was equally terrific when we became adults and she could share some of her wisdom, experience and humor. I think these late-night conversations were some of her favorite moments in the last two decades of her life.

―――――――――

One way Mom tried to make sure we would remain a strong family unit and remain close to each other was through our annual family reunion each summer. She started organizing these in the late 1990s, after Jerry had graduated from college and all of her children were independent adults. The first few years, we got together in Storm Lake, but then, she wanted to rotate the locations so a different family could host each year.

The 2008 family reunion was in St. Charles, Missouri, the home of my older brother Joe, his wife Cathy and their daughter Lauren. Joe and Cathy put together a tremendous reunion and we all had a blast. Each night of that weekend, the adults stayed up and visited. We have some great photos of Mom laughing during those conversations … and the discussions lasted until the early morning hours both nights.

After Mom and Dad returned home, she wrote the following email to her children:

Just a short note to let you know that the 'old folks' arrived home safely about 7 p.m., just in time to watch the Cubs. Hey, hey!!

Again, a wonderful gathering, and a very special thank you to Joe & Cathy for all their work and planning. And also, a big thank you to the 'big' kids for helping with the little ones, so the parents could have some reminiscing time. Those late-night conversations are sometimes very enlightening, especially for Grandma. I'm sure a great time was had by all.

Speaking of the Cubs, another great game. I hope those of you who were still on the road could get it on the radio. I'll bet Ronnie (Cubs' announcer Ron Santo) was going crazy. Go, Cubs, Go!!

Again, it was great to spend some time together. You'll never know how much I appreciate those times.

Love to you all. MOM

———————————

In the years since Mom died, we have continued having the annual family reunions each summer. We rotate the locations so different families continue to host. The nights usually run late with a group of us sitting up talking, sharing old stories, laughing and enjoying each other's company.

In the meantime, whenever I have a big decision to make, some news to share or something I want someone else's opinion about, my dad and my siblings are the first people I call.

We have a text group that my siblings and I use frequently to keep each other updated. We share all kinds of news, both good and bad.

We try to always be there for each other. It's a lesson that Mom taught repeatedly … and from where she's watching now, I hope she sees we are still following her lead.

CHAPTER 5

FRIDAY, JANUARY 2, 2009

D r. Williams comes by Mom's room at 7:30 a.m. for his daily visit and update. Again, the numbers and counts are not going in the right direction and it seems defeating. All seven of my siblings are here now and there is a feeling in the air unlike anything I have experienced. We are all happy to be together and everyone is bringing positive energy in conversations with Dad. We are all trying to lift Mom's spirits as much as possible. But sadness and helplessness are lurking just below the surface.

"What should we do now?" is the question we're asking ourselves. "What *can* we do?"

The answers seem fairly simple: spend time with Mom and Dad, make the best of the time that remains with Mom … and pray.

It's probably also time to let Mom's friends know what's going on. The last few days have rushed by so quickly, we haven't exactly communicated with other people very much. So I drive to my parents' house, which is a couple of blocks south of the hospital, and turn on Mom's computer. (Dad would never get within 20 feet of a computer, but Mom loved her emails, spreadsheets and internet research.)

At 9:38 a.m., I send the following email to Mom's address book:

This is Marty Gallagher writing from my mom's computer. I'm afraid the news isn't very good from here, but I wanted to send a note out to some of the people on Mom's email list to keep you informed.

Mom went into the hospital on Monday this week due to bronchitis, urinary tract infection and mild congestive heart failure. Each day, it seems that her energy has dipped and her numbers/counts are not going in the right direction. Yesterday, she was awake probably four or five times for 5 to 10 minutes each. This morning, her numbers were slightly down again. They are going to do a liver scan and a chest x-ray this morning, and we are guessing that those results will confirm our fears that the cancer is back and has spread.

I don't think that there is much time remaining for Mom and I think she was aware of that, given all the things she did to make this year's Christmas a special one for all of us (as she always has done).

All the family has been here since yesterday. Dad is doing pretty well.

I wish that I had better news to report and who knows, maybe we'll see a positive corner turned sometime today. Either way, please send some prayers Mom's direction. I know that you are all very special to her.

I will try to keep you posted. Thanks, Marty

I have a few errands to run, so I drive uptown to drop some things off at the post office and grab a few things at the grocery store. I enjoy listening to music when I'm driving, and I realize I haven't listened to music at all this week. Not once. I haven't had time and I haven't been in the mood. But, I turn on my car radio to give it a shot and see if it will pick up my spirits a bit.

The first song I hear is "Small Town" by John Cougar Mellencamp. It takes my mind to growing up in Strawberry Point and all the great things about living in a community that size. The next song is "Our House" by Madness, an upbeat song that shouldn't elicit an emotional response. But it hits me hard … especially with lyrics like this:

"Father gets up late for work

"Mother has to iron his shirt

"Then she sends the kids to school

"Sees them off with a small kiss

"She's the one they're going to miss

"In lots of ways."

I turn the station, trying to regroup and gather myself. The first song on the next station is "Heaven" by Bryan Adams.

Seriously.

Within five seconds, I turn the car radio off. I don't want music right now. And I think it's going to be a while.

———————————

This afternoon, Katie and Dad are in the room with Mom when the surgeon, Dr. Matthews, arrives to discuss what he sees on her scans and various reports. Mom is awake, although probably a little foggy from the pain meds.

"I wish I had good news, but I don't," the surgeon says. "The cancer is back and it has spread to your liver and bones." He shares a few sentences of explanation, but everyone in the room understands what he's saying.

Mom responds matter-of-factly. "Well, isn't that a kick in the head," she says.

It is the news we all suspected was coming, but there isn't a good way to brace yourself for it.

———————————

I have forwarded Mom's email contact list to my computer at home, so I open my email to send out another update. I'm surprised to find several responses already to my previous email … including a handful from people who found out as others were forwarding the information. I print several of these emails, hoping to read some of them to Mom later.

At 4:28 p.m., I email the following update to our growing list of family and friends:

Quick update on Mom...

Just wanted to keep you posted and let you know that our fears were realized today as the tests showed that the cancer is now in Mom's liver and spine. We are continuing to pray and trying to keep her as comfortable as possible.

Thanks for all your kind and thoughtful words and prayers.

This evening, Mom has been moved to a larger room, so Dad, my siblings and I are able to spend time in her new room with her. I sit in a chair next to Mom's bed and tell her we've been receiving a lot of emails offering support and prayers for her … and several from her former students – and parents of her former students – who are reaching out to share messages with her. She raises her eyebrows in surprise and I read about a dozen emails to her, including messages like these:

From a student named Kyle…

Dear Mrs. Gallagher, I wanted to share a few memories from kindergarten in the spring of 1985.

We were in our classroom in Strawberry Point, and all of us were huddled around, seated on the floor (on

carpet squares?) by the piano. It must have been St.
Patrick's Day and you were playing some songs for us.
"When Irish Eyes Are Smiling" sticks out in my head
because I have this distinct memory of you looking
directly at me and smiling ... and I was trying to look
through your glasses to see if those Irish eyes were, in
fact, smiling. They were. Well, I figured they had to
be Irish if you were singing a song about them. But
they certainly were bright. And if eyes could smile, I
thought, that's what it must look like.

Now that I think about it, the kindergarten year is so
important to begin a long career in school. I started
it in the best way possible: in a classroom with you
as a caring teacher. The image of your smiling eyes
will remain with me for my whole life, and for that I
am grateful. Thank you for all of the enduring ways
that you taught and cared for me, and the ways in
which you have taught and cared for all your students
throughout the years.

From a student named Abbie...

Hanging in my grandma's basement are the crowning
glory of kindergarten with Mrs. Gallagher – the alpha-
bet pants. My older sister hung 'her pants' (the size of
tag board with your height and weight at the top and
the letters of the alphabet around the seams) several

years before me – I was so jealous. I knew I was a big girl too when I got to hang my pants next to hers!

Mrs. Gallagher was a kind, yet firm teacher. She gave me a great start to learning, which I appreciate so much!

From a student named Ski…

Hello Mrs. Gallagher, I want you to know that you were always my favorite teacher and want to share some memories. In kindergarten we learned our numbers and letters off of a big pair of cardboard pants. Then we got to take them home, I tried to wear mine. We learned baseball from just about all of your boys. In fifth grade we would always get off the bus and come to your classroom and play Oregon Trail. You explained to us what dysentery was.

I hope you know how much you have meant to so many people from the Starmont area and I am sure Storm Lake as well. You are in our thoughts and prayers. We love you.

From a student named Jeremy…

I would like to express my gratitude to your mother. If she recalls I was a handful at one point in my life but I was fortunate enough to have a teacher (your mother) that never brushed me to the side or left me behind. Your mother has had an impact on so many people in her life and every student, friend and family member is better today because of her.

Strangely enough I can remember learning to tie my shoes on her flip chart using the Starmont shoe strings, along with story time and a piano. It is amazing the things that I remember from my days in your mother's class when I stop to think about them. Your mother is and always will be a wonderful woman.

From a parent named Julie...

Anne was our very first contact with a school teacher as new parents. I left Matt in her room in 1985 and walked down the empty hall, thinking, 'what is happening here? I just gave my child over to a huge (relative to our living room) public school system!' Your Mom had such a positive 'take charge' attitude, I knew he was in the most capable of hands! No child had a chance to be fretful, because she steered their bodies and minds where they needed to go before they knew what was happening, always three steps ahead of them!

She is an exceptional teacher in every way: very loving and demonstrative, kind, friendly, fun and motherly, and at the same time very organized, disciplined, challenging, goal-oriented and one who commands respect. Never underestimate the impact your mother's life has had and will continue to have on the lives of hundreds of children from this small rural community in middle America.

I read each email to her word for word and she loves every second of it. She is not one to get too sentimental, but her smile and her eyes tell me these messages mean a great deal to her.

The Lesson: The measure of one's life is not how many "things" one accumulates, but rather the number of lives he or she touches in a positive way. Mom had been a teacher for a large portion of her adult life and she was learning the powerful impact she truly had on so many people.

The memories of kindergarteners from a quarter-century ago came rushing back and I believe it brought her feelings of happiness, pride, comfort and peace. She knew she was a good teacher who cared deeply about her students, and it was such a treasure for so many of them to share their feelings and memories with her.

I don't think we can measure what those emails, which we continue to receive for several days, mean to Mom in her final week. But it sure reinforces the idea that you should tell the people you love that you love them. Share your feelings of respect, admiration and love with the people who mean a great deal to you. You'll never go wrong bringing this kind of warmth and light into someone's life, whether they are in a tough situation or not.

Although Mom's eyes aren't open all that often this evening, she smiles as she listens to Dad and their eight children talk, share stories and laugh. A handful of our favorite stories are re-told again as they seem to always draw some laughter.

I used to prank phone call my dad from time to time. The goal was to get him to say or do something ridiculous, or handle an absurd request ... and Mom's laughter was always the big payoff. For example, my two younger brothers, Ed and Jerry, had paper routes when they were in high school. They delivered the Des Moines Register to dozens of homes in several Storm Lake neighborhoods for a few years.

So, I share the story about when I called Dad one afternoon and disguised my voice as an elderly man, asking Dad, "Could you please have your boys bring the paper into my house each morning and put it on our kitchen table?"

Dad replied patiently, "No, I don't think the boys can do that. They're just supposed to drop it off inside the front door. That's the policy."

I pushed past that and continued, "Well, Edith and I would really appreciate it if they would bring it inside the house, put it on our kitchen table ... and open up the sports page for me while I'm eating my breakfast. That would be very helpful and we'd really appreciate it. Our front porch is a little chilly in the morning and we are still in our robes."

I could hear Mom in the background, asking Dad who it was and what was going on. I had identified myself as John Simons and told him my wife Edith and I live on Barton Street.

When Dad shared that information with Mom, she said, "The boys don't even deliver on *Barton Street* … that's not on their route."

Dad said to me, "I'm sorry, Mr. Simons, but Barton Street isn't even on my boys' route. It must be someone else delivering your paper."

I replied, "Aren't your boys the tall, skinny lad … and the other one looks just like Beaver from 'Beaver Cleaver?'"

"Yes, that's them," Dad said, sounding completely defeated.

As I tell that story to my siblings, Mom's smile grows wide. Dad laughs out loud. And there are a dozen other stories where Dad is the focal point of the prank.

Everyone knows which story is coming next.

It was early December of 1991 and I had graduated from Buena Vista University the previous spring. My brother Tim and I shared an apartment in town as we both worked at the local newspaper, The Storm Lake Times. Ed, a senior, and Jerry, a sophomore, were in high school at that time and Dad had recently turned 67.

Ed and Jerry were in Dad's basement one Saturday afternoon, watching a football game with Dad, when the phone rang at about 5 p.m.

Dad answered. The voice on the line sounded like an elderly woman and said, "Hi, this is Olga Burhop. We got a little snow this afternoon and I'm wondering if you and the boys could come shovel my driveway."

Dad waved to Ed and Jerry, pointed at the phone and whispered to the boys, "*It's Marty!*"

Then, Dad said to the person on the phone, "Well Olga … I don't think we got very much snow. I think you can probably handle it yourself." Dad started to chuckle, while Ed and Jerry listened intently to what might happen next.

The woman's voice responded, "Well, I'm hoping to go to church in about 20 minutes and was just hoping you could help clean off my driveway, so I can back out my car."

Dad said, "I don't think it's really all that bad. How about you throw on a pair of boots and give it a try yourself?"

At this point, Ed and Jerry are laughing … and Dad is LOVING it. As the voice on the phone is saying something, Dad is looking at Ed and Jerry, nodding along and waiting for his opening.

Then Dad says, "I'll tell you what Olga … Why don't you take that shovel and shove it right up your ass!" Then he immediately hangs up the phone, looks at Ed and Jerry and says, "I *finally got him!*"

They all share a good laugh. But it only lasts about 10 seconds, because that's when someone else walks into the room … *me*. Keep in mind this was before cell phones, so there is no chance I could've been the caller. Ed and Jerry looked at each other and start laughing harder and louder than maybe they ever have before, as they realize what has happened.

Dad turns a shade of pale that seems inhuman as he rips the phone book from a shelf to his right. As he thumbs through the pages, he's saying, "Burhop ... Burhop ... *Burhop* ..." And then, "Oh no," he says. And slowly dials the phone.

Ed and Jerry have tears streaming down their faces at this point, laughing uncontrollably. Dad, who is clearly rattled, says into the phone, "Hi Mrs. Burhop, this is Don Gallagher ... I've got this son, you see, and he's always trying to pull a fast one on me. I'm very sorry..."

The woman responds, "Well, I was really taken aback by the way you spoke to me."

Dad says, "I'm sorry. We'll be right over to shovel your driveway. And there will be no charge."

As I'm telling this story to my Dad and siblings in the hospital room and get to the part that Dad realizes there is actually an Olga Burhop and she only lives about three blocks away, Mom laughs out loud. A quick laugh, but loud. Her eyes are barely open, but this is a story that always gets her to laugh.

In that moment, Mom's hospital room is filled with joy.

The Lesson: Laughter can be the best medicine. Today has been a long day and the updates haven't been encouraging. But getting together with the people you love and sharing some laughs is a wonderful way to lift your spirits, gain a little strength and start to feel better, even if only for a while. This is something our family has consistently found to be the case, with the sound of Mom's laughter always the high point.

My mom and her family in 1950. From left: Everett, Bill, Anne, Tom and Cyrilla Stock. Mom was 14 years old when this photo was taken.

Mom teaching kindergarten in Algona, Iowa in 1958. This was her first teaching job.

Mom and Dad got married on August 5, 1961. Dad told me nearly 60 years later,
"The best decision I ever made was marrying Anne."

The Gallagher family in 1977. From left: Marty, Joe, Dan, Tim, Katie, Mom, Maggie (in back), Jerry (on Mom's lap), Dad and Ed.

Mom and Maggie when my older sister graduated from Starmont High School in May 1980. Mom taught preschool in our home in those days. When Mom returned to the classroom as a kindergarten teacher in the fall of 1981, Maggie took over as the teacher for "Strawberry Sprouts" preschool.

Mom and Dan when he graduated from high school in May 1983.

The Gallagher family in 1979. Front row, left to right: Tim, Marty, Jerry, Katie and Ed. Back row, left to right: Dan, Dad, Mom, Maggie and Joe.

Mom and Leo Gallagher (no relation) sat together at our sporting events when we were growing up. Dad would move around from one spot to another, visiting with people and occasionally giving a referee a hard time. This photo was taken in the fall of 1982, when Dan quarterbacked the Starmont football team to its first-ever state playoff appearance.

Mom and Joe dancing together on his wedding day on July 2, 1994.

The Gallagher family on Maggie's wedding day on July 21, 1984. Front row, left to right: Ed, Mom, Dad, Jerry. Back row, left to right: Tim, Katie, Dan, Joe, Marty, brother-in-law Al, Maggie.

Mom holding her granddaughter Lauren (Joe and Cathy's daughter) in December 2000.

Mom and Dad prepare to cut the cake at a party celebrating their 25th wedding anniversary in 1986.

Mom and Tim traveled from Storm Lake to our hometown of Strawberry Point in the early 2000s. They took several trips together as part of Chuck Offenburger's tours across the state of Iowa. Mom and Tim made numerous new friends on these trips and always had great fun.

Mom and Dad with Tim (far right) and me, while we were students at Buena Vista University in 1990.

Mom and Dad visit with me during a Parents' Night recognition prior to a Storm Lake High School basketball game in February 1995. Mom attended every one of the 206 games I coached from the fall of 1992 through the spring of 2000. Dad missed one game, so he could attend a friend's funeral.

Mom, Dad and me at our family reunion in August 2007. Our family wore matching t-shirts that year that Mom ordered for everyone.

Mom and Katie. This photo was taken during a celebration of our parents' 40th wedding anniversary in the summer of 2001.

Mom and Katie laughing. Mom's laugh is one of my all-time favorite sounds.

Ed and Mom. Two decades earlier, Ed just wanted Mom to give him a ride to the park.

Mom and Jerry. This photo was taken in December 2005. Mom's hair was short as a result of her chemotherapy treatments.

The Gallagher family in 1989. Front row, left to right: Katie, Dad, Mom, Jake (Maggie's son) and Maggie. Back row, left to right: Ed, Tim, Joe, Jerry, Marty, Dan and Al (Maggie's husband).

Dad and Mom dancing together.

My son Ben with Mom in February 2008. Ben and Mom had a lot of fun together. They shared a love of music. Ben performed "concerts" for her multiple times per week, singing and dancing in her living room.

Dad and Mom, holding grandsons Grady (left) and Paul (right). They are the oldest children of Tim and Jill.

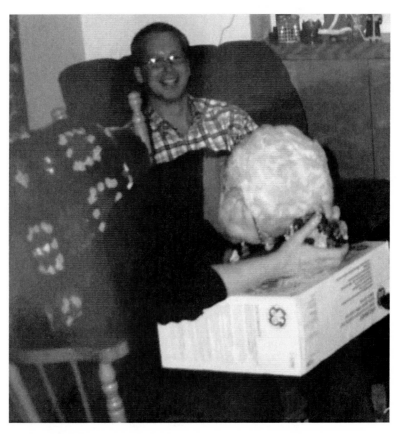

Mom doubles over laughing at something ridiculous, while opening a Christmas present. Dan is in the background. Laughter was always prevalent in our house.

After Mom's last day of teaching in May 2001, she prepares to eat dessert. Mom loved chocolate and definitely had a sweet tooth.

After Mom's last day of teaching in May 2001, we went out for a celebratory lunch together. Pictured, left to right: Dad, Jerry, Mom, Juli Kwikkel, Marty and Tim.

To celebrate Mom and Dad's 40th wedding anniversary in the summer of 2001, we had a party at Buena Vista University in Storm Lake. In this photo, Mom and Dad are listening to one of the speakers tell a story about them.

Mom and Dad share a hug at their 40th wedding anniversary party in the summer of 2001. Tim is in the background.

On Mom's birthday on February 8, 2008, Molly and Ben surprised her by making breakfast for her. They also made birthday cards for her, which Mom always loved to receive.

On Molly's birthday in October 2008, Mom gave Molly a hat that Mom crocheted for her. Molly thanked her with a hug and a kiss.

On December 20, 2008, Mom held her six-week-old grandson, Kinnick (Jerry's son). Our entire family gathered together that weekend to celebrate Christmas, which was Mom's favorite holiday.

Mom crocheted afghans for each of her 23 grandchildren in 2008 and handed them out as Christmas presents. Each afghan included the grandchild's name and high school graduation year. In this photo, Mom gives Erin (Ed's daughter) her afghan. Lauren (Joe's daughter) and Sarah (Maggie's daughter) are in the background.

Mom and Lucy (Katie's daughter) pose for a photo in December 2008. Lucy is holding her new graduation afghan that Mom crocheted for her.

This is the last photo taken of Mom. It was Christmas Day, 2008 and she was reading something Molly had written for her. Mom was encouraging her and making suggestions, always teaching.

This is a photo of my family in May 2018. Left to right: Molly, Carly, Sophie, Emily, Leo, Marty and Ben. One of the reasons I wrote this book was to introduce my mom to Emily, Carly, Sophie and Leo.

Don and Anne Gallagher, two of the greatest parents ever.

CHAPTER 6

SATURDAY, JANUARY 3, 2009

There is a sense of finality this morning that didn't exist in the last few days. I'm not sure exactly *when* something is going to happen, but it seems like the sands are moving through the hourglass at an accelerated pace.

I decide to talk to Molly and Ben and let them know what is going on. I don't want them to be caught completely off guard if something happens soon and they aren't at all prepared for it. I recognize they are only eight and five years old, so there is only so much they can understand and process, but they are very close to their grandma.

We sit down on the couch together in our living room. Molly is on my left and Ben on my right. They can tell the mood is serious and something is wrong. I explain to them that Grandma Gallagher is probably not going to get better. Ben starts to cry first … then Molly … and I struggle to keep it together.

"God is ready for Grandma Gallagher to join Him in Heaven, I think," I tell the kids. "And Grandma's body is tired and ready to rest."

The kids are hugging me now, burying their heads in my sides as I have one arm wrapped around each of them.

"But when that happens, Grandma Gallagher will always be with us," I explain. "She will still be able to watch you and try to help you from her special place in Heaven. And she will *always* love you."

This conversation is just as difficult as I imagined it would be.

"While she's still with us, though, we should spend time with her and let her know how much we love her," I say to the kids as they look at me and nod. We decide to go see her together in a little bit. I suggest the kids make cards for her to take with us. "She will love that," I tell them.

After a long hug with each of the kids, I grab some paper, pencils and colors for them to create their cards. The kids sit down at the dining room table, each making something special for their grandma.

The Lesson: Spend time with your children. Although this was a difficult conversation to have with Molly and Ben, it was important they hear this from me. They trusted me. And I knew their personalities well enough to know how to deliver such terrible news in a way that they could also feel supported. I hoped making cards would be a good outlet for them.

These are lessons I picked up from Mom by watching her parent her own kids … and witnessing her with her grandchildren the last couple of decades. Mom had a way of making each child feel special. Each child knew they were a priority around Mom. And they *knew* they were loved.

Over the lunch hour, I take the kids to the hospital so they can give the cards they've made to their grandma. Mom's eyes are open when we walk in the room. She is so happy to see Molly and Ben. She greets them with a big smile and a hello, almost as if she finds an extra level of strength for the kids.

Molly walks right up to Mom's bed and shows her the card she made. Mom loves it, of course, and smiles. Mom engages Molly in a conversation about the picture she drew and compliments her repeatedly for her artwork. She asks Molly about what she's been working on in school the last couple of days.

Ben, who is only five and is very soft-hearted, wants *me* to give Mom his card and he refuses to come to her bedside. Mom's condition has changed dramatically since Ben saw her on Wednesday night, less than three days ago. It's sad and scary for a five-year old to comprehend. Mom smiles and compliments Ben for his card too. She asks him about his music and if he's performed any concerts recently. Ben smiles briefly, but he is too heartbroken to talk.

Mom visits for a few more minutes. Then she thanks the kids for coming, blows them each a kiss and tells them she loves them.

I hold the kids' little hands as we walk out of the room and down the hallway. My eyes are welling with tears as we leave. Molly and Ben don't know it, but this was their good-bye to Grandma Gallagher.

The Lesson: Encourage your children and take an interest in *their* interests. One of the reasons Mom had a special relationship with my kids was because she always encouraged them in whatever they were interested in doing.

Whether it was sports, reading, performing, drawing, painting, writing, dancing, magic or something else, Mom always made her children and grandchildren feel like they could be successful. She always wanted to help each child find his or her passion. "If you love what you do, you'll never work a day in your life," Mom often said.

She was supportive, always providing positive feedback. But she also asked questions, digging deeper, which showed the kids her support was sincere. Mom used to tell me that kids could always spot a "phony" or a "fake." This is probably another big reason she was so tremendous with kids and such a wonderful teacher. Her interest and support were always genuine.

The results were not only terrific relationships between her and the kids, but the kids would feel greater confidence and a desire to keep pushing. A little encouragement goes a long way, something Mom proved repeatedly with dozens – no, *hundreds* – of children through the years.

This afternoon, I check my email at home and there are dozens more emails for Mom. Some from family, others from friends, many from former students … and when I compile them into one file and print them out, there are more than 40 pages of messages for her.

I put these in a folder and take them with me when I return to the hospital. She loves hearing these thoughts and memories from such a wide variety of people in her life. I try to reply to each person who sends a message, thanking them for taking the time to write something. But they'll never know the impact it makes for Mom.

This evening, Dad, my siblings and I stay in Mom's room again, visiting and trading stories. The sound of laughter is a constant. Mom's eyes are closed for much of the night, but her smile and occasional laugh tell us she is doing her best to listen.

At one point, someone says we should leave and let Mom get some sleep. "No," she says quietly. "This is great. Please stay … I'm enjoying this."

So we stay. And the stories and laughs continue.

I share with my siblings that I've taken Mom to several movies in the last decade, including "Saving Private Ryan," "For Love of the Game," "Thirteen Days" and "Charlie Wilson's War," among others.

I tell them about one of the first scenes in "Charlie Wilson's War," which shows the Tom Hanks character sitting in a hot tub with a couple of topless women. As I'm sitting next to my mother, I'm a little uncomfortable … Should I look away? Close my eyes? Stop eating my popcorn? Eat *more* popcorn? Just hope the scene ends? After all, I'm sitting next to the woman who wouldn't let us watch "Three's Company" on TV in the late 1970s because it was, in her words, "a jiggle show."

Then I share a story about taking Mom to "Saving Private Ryan." We were sitting in the middle of a packed theater and the first 20 minutes of that movie are as intense as any movie I've ever seen. It is an edge-of-your-seat story filmed so realistically, the people in the theater are absolutely locked in. The tension is thick. About halfway into the movie, Ted Danson emerges as a U.S. Army Captain discussing the mission of finding Private Ryan. In the middle of the dialogue, Mom leans over to me and says in a voice loud enough for anyone within 20 feet to hear, "Hey … that's the guy from '*Cheers!*'"

Everyone in the hospital room laughs, including Mom. It wasn't like Mom to talk too loud or ever draw attention to herself. And I liked to tease her that she just took 50 people out of the experience of World War II and got them thinking about Norm and Cliff sitting at a bar.

One of Mom's favorite stories comes up later and even though we've all heard it before, it's another one that always gets a laugh from Mom. It was a summer day in 1970 … Mom and Dad had five kids at the time (Maggie was 7, Dan was 5, Joe was 3, Tim was 2, I was almost a year) and Mom was pregnant with Katie.

In those days, kids played outside and figured out their own games.

On this particular day, Dan and Joe were off by themselves in the backyard. Mom was in the kitchen, getting lunch ready when Joe came running in the house through the back door. He was clearly wet and he smelled awful … but he appeared to be excited.

"What in the world have you been doing?" Mom asked Joe.

"Danny has been teaching me how to pee straight up," he said. "And I *finally did it!*"

Mom shakes her head and laughs. Raising six boys presented its challenges … and she was there for all the shenanigans. Or at least, a lot of them.

Another summer day, this one in 1975, the four oldest boys (Dan, Joe, Tim and me) got into trouble for something we were doing outside. Mom was very unhappy about it, which didn't happen often. She brought us inside and made us go upstairs into our bedroom (yes, *all four of us* shared a room) and she locked the door from the outside, using the latch that was a handy way of keeping us contained.

It was such a beautiful, sunny day and the four of us just wanted to get back outside and play. We needed to figure out a plan. Mom was doing laundry, so she was probably back down in the basement, while we were locked in our bedroom on the second floor.

A unique thing about the house we grew up in was that we had a clothes chute in our bedroom that went all the way to the basement. But it also had an opening on the main floor, where Maggie's room was located.

So we decided to hook together several belts and hang them down the clothes chute. Then, we stuffed Tim (who was the smallest at the time) into the clothes chute to climb down the belts. The plan was for him to climb out on the main floor, run upstairs to unlock our door … and we could all escape to go back outside to play.

Seemed like a good idea. Until it wasn't.

Unfortunately, Tim got stuck about halfway down and all the commotion alerted Mom to what was happening. Before we got Tim all the way back out of the clothes chute, Mom opened the door and gave us our second earful of the day.

Mom loves this story. And we all wonder how she kept a straight face when she realized what we were trying to do. But that's a skill that only a great parent can master.

When I was eight years old, I started making cards for Mom on her birthday and Mother's Day. I would use two or three sheets of paper, folded over … and include a poem and illustrations. The poem always made fun of different events from the past year, but the final punchline was *always* a shot at Dad for being "cheap."

I doubt that I had a complete understanding of being cheap when I was eight, but I knew one thing: it made Mom laugh. After one or two of these holidays, Mom started waiting to read my card until the very end, after she had opened her presents. And she would read the cards out loud for everyone, stopping a few times to laugh out loud, which inevitably led the rest of us to laugh too.

Everyone knew there was a jab at Dad coming at the end. But we all laughed anyway, mostly because Mom was laughing so hard.

Eventually, I started making these cards for Dad on his birthday and Father's Day, but it was *still* Mom who got to read them out loud.

The Lesson: Laugh loud. Mom had the greatest laugh. She would tip her head back, her chuckle would grow to a howl until tears would start to roll down her cheeks. It was contagious. When she was laughing, you couldn't help but laugh with her. And there are very few things better than a room full of laughter.

One more story is told about a summer day in the 1970s, probably around 1978. Mom is working on several things at once, neck-deep doing what would later be termed "multi-tasking." All the Gallagher kids are busy doing something – and not "underfoot" as Mom would say – except Ed, who is about five years old.

Ed desperately wants to go to the city park to play. He asks Mom if she can drive him to the park. She tells him, "No, not right now."

Like all five-year old boys, Ed persists. He asks again. And again. And *again*. "Mom, will you take me to the park?"

After turning him down for the umpteenth time – and trying to get several things done at once – Mom hits her breaking point. "Eddy, if you ask me *one more time* to take you to the park, you're going to drive me to a mental institution!" she says.

Without missing a beat, Ed responds, "Would you drop me off at the park on the way?"

Again, laughter fills the room.

The Lesson: Spend time together, share stories and laughter. This may seem obvious, but these moments when we are sharing stories and making each other laugh are some of the greatest times we spend together. The best stories never get old. Retelling these stories can be the best way to document those moments so they aren't forgotten and future generations can enjoy the laughs, as well.

CHAPTER 7

SUNDAY, JANUARY 4, 2009

Tim and Joe spent the night in Mom's room last night, and I know Dad and others are there with her early this morning. She has plenty of company. So, I decide to spend a little time at home working on something to share with Mom later today.

I get on my computer and find my favorite photos of Mom from the past year. These include pictures of her with Dad, with the kids, on Christmas … a variety of special times and great memories. I don't have a lot of time to spend, so I know the finished product will be pretty rudimentary, but I know Mom won't care about that.

I print each photo out on its own page – 42 of them in all – and then put a front and back cover on it (green construction paper). I bind it all together with a spiral binder and give it the title of "The Grandma Book."

The Lesson: Be creative. Mom always encouraged us to create things, whether it was through writing, drawing, painting or some other outlet. She loved hand-made gifts the most. This was a lesson that Mom taught us through her examples as much as through her words.

Whenever she was at home watching a Cubs game or a Hawkeye game on TV, she was often also crocheting an afghan for someone. One day I stopped by their house and Mom was crocheting an afghan, while watching a DVD of HBO's R-rated comedy/drama "Sex and the City." When I walked in the room, she was startled and hit the "stop" button on the remote.

"Oh geez," she said. "I thought you were your father. He wouldn't like that I'm watching this show at all." I told Mom her secret was safe with me and we laughed about it. She was never wasting time, even when she was watching TV.

Mom would make personalized afghans for people when they graduated from high school or college, when they got married and for their children. She would ask them what pattern and colors they liked, and then crochet the most terrific, colorful afghans. Mom also had some standard patterns she would use to keep a few on hand, just in case she needed one quickly. Each adult-sized, personalized afghan would take her 40 hours to create.

In the first 11 months of 2008, Mom made an additional 23 afghans, one high school graduation afghan for each of her grandchildren. Each of these afghans included the child's name and graduation year. She completed them all and wrapped them as Christmas presents. It was an amazing scene at her house when we celebrated Christmas, with all the grandchildren and their afghans, including one for six-week old Kinnick Gallagher, who was born on November 8, 2008.

Mom was right, the hand-made gifts are always the best.

———————————

Jerry told me last night that he planned to leave this morning as he has a six-hour drive back to his home in Eau Claire, Wisconsin where he is a television news anchor. He recently turned 33 years old and is the youngest of my siblings. Jerry is smart, driven, empathetic and funny. We've always been close.

I call Jerry to see if he is still around. He is already on the road, driving home. He left the hospital around 10 a.m. I ask him how things went before he left. He tells me he wanted some time alone with Mom this morning, so he essentially kicked Tim, Joe and Dad out of her room.

"I pulled up a chair and sat right beside her and held her hand," Jerry says. "We talked for about 15 minutes and it was very good. I knew this might be the last time I would see her, but I wasn't sure if *she* knew that I wouldn't be coming back. But when we were done talking, I stood up to lean in and give her a hug ... and she sat right up. *She knew.*

"We hugged. I told her I love her and she said she loved me too."

Jerry pauses for a few seconds.

"When I walked out of her room, I couldn't look back. I walked into the hallway and Dad and Tim were standing there. I had tears coming down my face and gave Dad a hug."

Jerry pauses again, this time for 10 or 15 seconds, fighting back his emotions.

"I told him I just don't want to see her suffer. He hugged me back.

"I've never seen Tim cry, but he turned to the left and walked down the hallway to look out the window," he says. "It was probably getting to be too much. I just wanted to get in my car and drive home, so I headed out.

"But I'm so glad that I got that time with her."

Mom has less pain and nausea today, which allows her to sit up and visit with people several times throughout the day. She even gets up and sits in the recliner beside her bed for about 90 minutes this afternoon. Mom says she absolutely loved listening to all the stories last night and having everyone together.

Unfortunately, a few more of my siblings need to return to their homes. There is a light snow and a little rain in the forecast, so we hope the road conditions won't be an issue. Or maybe we're just discussing the weather because nobody wants to say what most of us are really thinking.

This is likely the final good-bye to Mom for at least two more siblings, Dan and Joe. I don't see Dan before he leaves, but I see Joe walk out of the room after he talks with Mom. Joe is

41 years old and I don't think I've seen him cry since we were little boys. It's heartbreaking.

"Mom seemed well enough that we were hopeful when we left," Dan tells me later. "The last thing I said to her – which I rarely ever said, but I am glad I did – I told her I loved her and she told me she loved me too."

Later this afternoon, it's my turn to spend time with Mom. We talk about a variety of things. Mom and I are very close. We've had countless deep conversations about life, people, goals, religion and raising children. She knew my strengths and celebrated them, and she knew my weaknesses … but she always loved me anyway.

As I look at her now, in her hospital bed and battling physical pain she doesn't discuss, memories rush at me. I was three years old and she was so proud that I could read headlines and parts of stories in a newspaper. I was five and she started teaching me to play the piano. I was in junior high and really made her angry a couple of times. I was in high school and she seemed to trust me to make good decisions. Throughout my adult life, she was my go-to person for advice or to share positive news.

Throughout her battle with cancer, I had tried to always be there for her. From her initial appointments with the doctor almost three years earlier, through the chemotherapy and radiation treatments, and eventually what seemed like a recovery for a couple of years.

By any measure, given her initial diagnosis, having Mom remain with us the last few years was a miracle.

I was a single parent of two small children who lived four blocks away. The number of times Mom was there for me in the last few years to lend a hand – or an ear – was incalculable. There are times I believe God gave us a couple of extra years with Mom because He knew I needed her. So did Molly and Ben.

As we sit there in her hospital room talking, I do my best to hold it together.

I show her "The Grandma Book" I put together earlier today. With each page, we talk about the photo and the story it represents.

There's a photo of Mom and Ben on her living room floor, sorting through CDs as they decide which songs to listen to next. A photo of Ben making slime in Mom's kitchen. A picture of Mom, Dad, Molly and Ben the night we held an impromptu "Father-Daughter Dance" at their house. A photo from Mom's birthday – last February – when Molly and Ben fixed breakfast for her.

A picture of Molly and Ben sitting with Mom and Dad, everyone holding little paper puppets the kids made for a puppet show they performed. A photo of Molly playing Mom's piano. A picture of Mom and Dad, sitting with us at our dining room table last October on Molly's birthday.

A photo of Molly, wearing a cute hat Mom crocheted for her, as she's giving Mom a kiss on the cheek. A picture of the kids trick-or-treating at Mom and Dad's house as a ghost and Darth Vader. And on and on it goes. Mom's smile tells me this was well worth the effort.

Mom tells me how wonderful it was that everyone made it to see her this weekend and she was overjoyed to see all her kids. Then she raises her eyebrows and says, "Everyone has their own lives, their own jobs … and they all came here to see me…" Her voice trails off as if she's in disbelief.

"That's because we all love you so much," I tell her. "You shouldn't be surprised by that."

Mom smiles, closes her eyes and rests for a while.

Seeing everyone really did warm her heart in a way that I'm sure none of us can know or understand in this moment. Mom seems to be in a really happy, appreciative place right now, despite what she is facing.

After about 20 minutes, she opens her eyes again. I ask her if she wants to hear some of the email messages we've received in the last 24 hours. She says "Sure" and again seems to be incredulous that people are making this effort for her. We share laughs as I read emails to her and she says she feels a little "overwhelmed" by how much love is being expressed for her.

"You deserve every bit of it," I tell her.

Dad comes into the room at 6 p.m. and kicks me out. He wants some time alone with Mom. I return to Mom's room at 10 p.m. to spend the night and Dad hangs out with us for about 30 minutes before he heads home. It's been a long day, a very full day ... and in many ways, a very good day. I'm amazed at how long Mom stayed awake for it all and how much she was able to visit with everyone. Again, given her condition, that seems like a bit of a miracle.

The Lesson: Do everything you can to give comfort to the people you love. Even though Mom had to be exhausted, she felt it was important today to share her time with everyone ... and that these individual conversations needed to take place. She somehow mustered all the strength she could to make it happen. And I have no doubt these moments were more for *our* benefit than for Mom.

But she fought through her pain and sickness to give us each a chance to spend time with her, share stories, laughs and "I love yous." I hope it brought her some joy and comfort. I know the rest of us needed it.

CHAPTER 8

MONDAY, JANUARY 5, 2009

Mom was a little restless and requested a sleeping pill to help her get to sleep last night.

At around 7:30 a.m., Dr. Williams arrives at Mom's room. She tells the doctor her pain is about a seven (on a scale of 1 to 10), so he says he will increase her pain meds. Mom adds she is suffering from a little nausea as well, so Dr. Williams says he will address that too.

When the doctor leaves, I follow him to the hallway to ask a few follow-up questions. He says some of the same things we already know and I'm sure it's a tough spot for him trying to say the same things in different ways. Mom's white blood cell count is at about 17,000, which is probably due to her body trying to fight off the cancer. Dr. Williams says her liver function was a little better yesterday, which is puzzling to him.

The bottom line, though, is he thinks her cancer is spreading rapidly. "The main goals now are to keep her pain down and get rid of the nausea," he says.

The surgeon, Dr. Matthews, will likely stop by sometime today to talk about Mom's recent CT scan. And Mom has an appointment scheduled later today with her oncologist, who will be making the trip from Sioux City, which is about 70 miles west of Storm Lake.

Mom does take a sip of coffee this morning, which is the first sip she's had in about three weeks. She also had a little bit of a milkshake and a few sips on a combination of orange juice and Sierra Mist. In the moments she's awake, Mom is lucid and makes conversation with Dad and me. But those moments are getting fewer and farther between today, especially compared to how awake and alert she was this past weekend.

"I'm going to go home and catch up on some work," I tell Dad at 10 a.m. "But I'll come back at noon."

"Yes, stay on top of your work," Dad says. "I'll be fine here with Mom."

I'm sure he's right about that. I think about all the time Mom and Dad have spent together the last 47-plus years. They have had different roles in our family, but they also managed to carve out time to spend with each other.

They challenge each other, no doubt. They are both brilliant people, independent thinkers with a stubborn streak. They haven't seen eye-to-eye on *everything* the last half-century, but I think it would be weird if they did.

Ultimately, they love each other and share a tremendous amount of respect for each other.

The Lesson: Spend time with your spouse away from your kids. Despite the demands of raising eight children together, Mom and Dad always managed to break away for some time together as a couple. They would get a babysitter lined up and go out for dinner or drinks. Dad is more social than Mom, but there's a yin-and-yang to that, I'm sure. They each have a great sense of humor and love to laugh, so I'm sure they had plenty of fun together.

Mom and Dad also belonged to a bridge club in Strawberry Point. To the best of my knowledge, this was a group of four to six couples who got together to play cards, maybe once every couple of months. The club rotated who the host couple would be.

On the nights the bridge club met in our house, Mom and Dad would set up two or three card tables in our living room. I recall each table had an ashtray and a little bowl filled with green olives. The drinking glasses sitting out were ones we only used on special occasions (like maybe Christmas dinner). Before the guests arrived, all the kids were sent to bed early and nobody was allowed to interrupt. If either of my parents heard footsteps coming down the stairs, there would be trouble. I'm not sure this ever happened, but we seemed *certain* this was a line not to cross.

As kids, the four older boys (Dan, Joe, Tim and me) would sit together in the hallway upstairs and listen to the adults downstairs for a while. It seemed like several people talking at once, a lot of laughter, glasses clinking and the smells of perfume and cigarette smoke. After a few minutes of realizing it meant nothing to us, we would retreat to our room and discuss Hawkeye basketball, the Cubs or an upcoming little league opponent.

I return to the hospital over the noon hour and visit with Dad. He tells me Dr. Matthews stopped by a little earlier. "He was very good with Mom," Dad says. "He explained things and let her know they are doing what they can to ease the pain."

Dr. Matthews also told Dad that he believes the cancer is now in Mom's bones.

Mom is in a little more pain today, so they've increased the morphine ... and they have given her a little switch that's connected to her morphine drip, so when she needs more, she can get it.

The main thing is to minimize her pain and discomfort as much as possible. Her nausea isn't as bad as it was this morning.

Dad tells me that Mom was hallucinating a little bit earlier, telling him things that didn't make sense. But then, he says, she would snap out of it and converse normally again.

Katie went home to Cedar Falls yesterday, but she plans to return this afternoon for Mom's appointment with the oncologist. At 3:13 p.m., she sends an email to all the siblings. It says:

I wanted to relay that the other day Mom was hallucinating a bit when she was up in the chair. She said, 'Tell her the footstool is over there.' I asked her, 'What?' and she said, 'So Jesus can wash her feet … I wanted them to know it's over there, they were asking.' Then she snapped out of it and raised the cup to her lip and said, 'I'd better have some water and snap back to reality.' I thought this was neat/important in more ways than one.

I'm leaving as soon as I can get out the door. Bag is packed and work is done for the day … I'd like to make it there before the oncologist, but don't know if that's possible now.

Dad and I wait with Mom for the oncologist to arrive in her room. It's now almost 6 p.m. He's running late today. Mom has been asleep most of the afternoon and not very conversant in the brief moments she's awake.

The door opens. It's Katie. She walks in with just a minute to spare.

Then the oncologist, Dr. Crass (not his real name) arrives. He is wearing clothes that don't match and pants that are too short (as Katie would point out to me later), but his fashion sense is not the issue. He is just such a jerk.

Dr. Crass has an assistant with him, a woman in her 40s who appears used to being berated in front of people. She is carrying a stack of papers that has to be almost 400 pages thick. I would describe her as timid, but I'm pretty sure I see a little anger in her face too. She's undoubtedly seen it all.

The doctor blows past Dad, doesn't greet Katie or me in any way and walks right up to Mom's bedside. Mom's eyes are still closed and she's sleeping. Dr. Crass doesn't care. He just barks at her, "So, what's the problem?"

What's the *problem*? Are you SERIOUS? She's a 72-year old woman dying of cancer. What's the *problem*?!? What's YOUR problem?

Mom opens her eyes. "I have cancer," she says. "It's in my liver and my bones."

Dr. Crass grabs a stack of papers from his assistant and flips through them hastily, appearing angrier by the second. He grumbles something to his assistant, who then hands him some more papers.

"Who told you that you have cancer?" he says to Mom. I cannot imagine how he could be any more callous.

Dad starts to answer the question, but Mom says, "Dr. Matthews. He saw it in my scans."

Dr. Crass turns to his assistant and scoffs, "Not THESE!" shoving the papers back at his assistant, then repeats his earlier request. She hands him a different stack of papers.

He flips through these pages.

"Nothing in here tells me your cancer has returned," Dr. Crass says.

Never in my life have I heard someone deliver such potentially terrific news in a way that made everyone else in the room thoroughly disgusted. It was very confusing. What did he just say? Is it actually POSSIBLE that Mom's cancer has NOT returned?

The doctor continues to dispute the diagnosis previously delivered by both Dr. Williams and Dr. Matthews. He insists his belief is that the issue is her gall bladder, which he schedules to be removed on Wednesday at Mercy Medical Center in Sioux City.

It all happens so fast. And just like that, he storms out ... almost like a cartoon character, with dust trailing him. And a completely embarrassed assistant who probably hates her job most days.

As the door closes behind the oncologist, Dad, Katie and I look at each other. We are all puzzled, trying to determine if Dr. Crass knows what he is talking about while reconciling that concern with witnessing the absolute WORST bed-side manner we've ever seen.

We decide this is at least the *possibility* of good news. Maybe there's a chance Mom's issues are gall bladder-related. Maybe not. But it seems like it's worth a try. And if it brings a feeling of hope to a previously hopeless situation, how could we reject this option?

The entire situation was surreal. It's been a very long week. We are all exhausted … mentally, physically and emotionally. The doctor was late. Katie barely made it in time. The cancer diagnosis was questioned. Surgery was recommended for something we had not previously considered. And all the while, the doctor's behavior was positively boorish.

The Lesson: Be patient. It was not a time for us to show our annoyance or anger. We needed to remain calm and steady, sifting through the rubbish to see what was truly important in that moment. This is something Mom had become an expert at during her decades of raising her kids and leading a classroom.

In December 2005, I wanted to create something unique for Mom and Dad for Christmas. I emailed each of my siblings several different questions about growing up in Strawberry Point and seeking memories our parents would enjoy. The questions included "What was the worst job around the house while you were growing up?" and "What is your favorite 'family trip' story?"

The result was a 36-page book full of wonderful stories, hilarious situations and ridiculous comments with a thread of love woven throughout.

There were dozens of times in the next few years that I would stop over to my parents' house and Mom would be sitting in her chair, reading through that book. Often laughing. Always smiling.

The first question each of us answered was "What is your favorite 'Gallagher Family Christmas' memory?" Tim's answer to that question spelled out Mom's patience beautifully. Which makes perfect sense, because Tim has been honored multiple times by the Iowa Newspaper Association as Iowa's Best Newspaper Columnist. He has a fantastic way with words – both as a writer and as a speaker – and he is extremely adept at getting to the heart of any situation. (It's no wonder he's always been the "favorite!")

Here is Tim's answer about his Christmas memory:

My favorite holiday memory takes me back to the upstairs bathroom when I was probably six years old. I took my United States map puzzle and laid down on the upstairs bathroom floor (a thin green carpet ... and I can't imagine what it was soaked with over the years) and sobbed quietly.

Christmas is an emotional time for children. It is for everyone. But especially so for a child who focuses for more than a month on those prizes waiting to be opened. Coaches talk about players bringing another level of "energy" to a game. Can you imagine the level of "energy" Mom and Dad – primarily Mom, let's not kid ourselves – had to harness in the four weeks leading to our annual Christmas bonanza?

Undoubtedly, she also knew an emotional free-fall of sorts would transpire for at least one, if not two, of her children. I don't know if Dr. Spock wrote about such things, but that's the nature of children after a birthday, after an overnight stay.

For me, it was late Christmas night, about 1974. Gerald Ford was President and Anne Gallagher's "favorite" child was letting her down, crying and complaining that he didn't get the best presents in the world. Could it get any worse?

Rather than crack me with a spoon, I remember how she grabbed a seat on the toilet and listened. That's all. She listened. I'm sure she was frustrated as hell after having scrounged Oelwein, Manchester and Rima's Department Store for up to 200 gifts, wrapped and hid them all and still had someone complaining. Heck, there were probably others. This might have been the same year Marty gave everyone a little black comb. Who can forget that?

During my spell, I think I looked at her once. I couldn't bear to glance her way, not while talking about how other children fared better and basically laying it all on her, the very woman who fed me, clothed me, and now, at 11 p.m., counseled me with few words and an exhausted expression that likely conveyed disappointment, sympathy and humor, if that's a combination you can find. Then again, that's how many might describe the Ford Administration.

I rambled. I snuffled. I wiped my nose and eventually, I think, apologized, gave her a hug and told her how much I loved her. I haven't ever written about this, or told this to anyone ... and I'm choking up now as I write about it. It was a cold Christmas night more than three decades ago and the memory of her hug still has hold of me.

———————————

Mom wants to go forward with the surgery and have her gall bladder removed. It's obviously a risk, given her current situation. But she is definitely in favor. She is also the only person in the hospital room tonight who wasn't repulsed by the behavior and demeanor of the oncologist. Mom has described him before as pretty rough, but she's unfazed by it. She says she just wants the information and doesn't need – or want – to be coddled in any way.

I'm sure that's true, but there is a happy medium between being coddled and having someone bark, "What's the problem?" at you while you're barely conscious and on a morphine drip.

But that's Mom.

And so, we begin plans to get Mom transferred to Mercy Medical Center in Sioux City tomorrow for a Wednesday surgery to remove her gall bladder.

The Lesson: Keep your composure. Mom had a way of keeping her wits about her when people around her were losing theirs.

Few experiences made this any more evident than the rare occasion we would take a family trip.

We didn't take many family trips, with all 10 of us crammed into one vehicle. But when we did, it was usually worthy of a story later.

One Saturday in 1977, one of our cousins was getting married in Grinnell, Iowa. Mom and Dad decided we should all go to this event together. It would take about two hours to get to the church from our house. As usual, before we left, Mom gave Dramamine to the four or five kids who suffered from car sickness. I wasn't on that list, thankfully.

We piled into Dad's company van. Dad in the driver's seat, Mom in the other front seat. There were two rows of bench seats: Katie, Maggie and Tim in the back seat ... Dan, Joe and me in the first bench seat. Ed and Jerry laid down on the floor, side-by-side, under the seats. I'm not kidding. Their heads were between Mom's and Dad's seats and their bodies were under the bench seats. Although they were very little at the time: Ed was four years old and Jerry was two.

Our plan was to drive straight to the church, so all of us were already dressed up in our best outfits.

What could possibly go wrong?

Quite a bit, as it turns out.

We were on the road for about 30 minutes when Mom asked if the wedding gift was in the back, behind the last bench seat. Nobody could find it back there. Dad's mercury started rising immediately. He pulled the van over and we looked for the gift. It was nowhere to be found.

We had *forgotten* the wedding present. Dad was not happy … and he was vocal about it.

Dad turned the van around and we headed back for Strawberry Point. We were going to go back home, pick up the present … and arrive in Grinnell at the reception without anyone noticing we had missed the wedding. That last part seemed implausible with eight kids in our crew, but nobody was going to point that out to Dad in the moment.

Sure enough, the wedding gift was on the dining room table. Mom put it in the van and we hit the road. Again.

Dad felt like we had fallen behind schedule for getting to the reception in good shape. So he started driving a bit faster than before. When we were probably 45 minutes from arriving, Dad decided to take some back roads to get there a bit quicker. At some point, the back roads turned into a gravel road. The van began to shimmy a bit … and the ride got bouncy.

At this point, Ed announced that he had to pee. Mom asked him if he could hold it for a little while longer.

The older boys had a pretty good idea there was no chance that a four-year old was going to be able to hold it for a half-hour or so, in a bouncy ride. So at this point, Dan, Joe, Tim and I were watching and waiting to see what was going to happen next. And when the van began to start smoking a little from under the hood, we knew we were in for quite a show.

Dad ignored the smoke from the van. He kept forging ahead, maybe even a little quicker. Which made the ride bumpier. And he started talking to himself – about the van, about the gift – and became more and more agitated, even slipping in some colorful language. While the four older boys were feeling completely entertained, Maggie was not. She was an emotional teenager and she began to cry. Mom sent a Kleenex box back to Maggie.

"I really have to pee," Ed insisted.

Mom may have asked Dad if we could stop. Or she may have avoided that discussion, knowing full well the answer would be negative.

The drive continued. Bouncing along a gravel road at a speed that was probably not the greatest idea, but Dad was rolling the dice.

"I REALLY have to pee!" Ed said, as he stood up between Mom's and Dad's seats.

Mom grabbed the empty, one-gallon ice cream bucket we brought on every trip. It was usually the receptacle for any of the kids who get car sick if they need to vomit. Today, it would be a different kind of receptacle … and the older boys were watching this with tremendous anticipation.

As Dad continued to drive like we were in an emergency vehicle on our way to an accident scene, Mom held the ice cream bucket for Ed as he unzipped his pants. There was no turning back now. *This was happening.*

Ed had to pee, all right. And he peed A LOT. The problem was that he was peeing almost everywhere but in the bucket. It was on Mom's arm, her wrist, her dress, the dashboard, her seat … it was incredible. Mom was trying to both hold Ed upright *and* catch the pee in the bucket at the same time. No Olympic sport required the combination of dexterity, focus and coordination Mom displayed in that moment.

Four of us boys were laughing very loudly. It was uncontrollable … and there were comments flying around undeterred. Maggie was still crying. Ed was getting his pants zipped back up, trying not to fall down. Mom was holding a bucket with a little bit of pee inside it. And she calmly asked for the Kleenex box to be returned to her as she needed to clean herself off.

Ed laid back down, Mom tried to get cleaned off. The bucket was discarded out the window. The older boys were laughing. Dad was swearing. And Maggie was crying.

Then Katie spoke up.

"I don't feel very good," she said. "I think I'm going to throw up."

The puke bucket was no longer with us. Mom, thinking quickly, sent the Kleenex box back to the back seat.

Katie started puking into the Kleenex box. The four older boys were howling now, witnessing one of the greatest five-minute scenes we thought we'd ever see. Maggie was trying to help Katie. Ed and Jerry were trying to see what was happening from their vantage point on the floor. Dad was immune to it all …

driving in Grinnell at this point, on paved roads as he searched for the reception venue.

We arrived at the reception at about the same time as the wedding party. Everyone – and I mean, *everyone* – noticed our arrival as the 10 of us poured out of the van. Some of us had tears from laughing so much, others had tears from crying and you can bet the four older boys could not wait to share this story with some of our cousins.

Mom, somehow, managed to walk into the reception as calm and cool as ever. As if the drive to Grinnell was completely uneventful. A breeze.

Mom put on a master's class that afternoon on keeping her composure. It was amazing. And unforgettable.

CHAPTER 9

TUESDAY, JANUARY 6, 2009

Even with the morphine in her system, Mom continues to be in some pain today. But we hope the gall bladder surgery will provide some relief … and maybe some answers.

Dad, Katie and I are on the main floor of the hospital near the back entrance of the emergency room. This is where Mom is going to be taken out to an ambulance for the ride to Mercy Medical Center in Sioux City.

As we are meeting with the appropriate hospital staff and signing paperwork, the two-person ambulance crew approaches us. One of them asks us "What is her mentation?"

Mentation? It seems like such a weird word. Katie and I exchange a look. I'm sure it's a word – and I'm guessing we know what it means – but still.

"Are you asking if she's conscious?" Katie says and then answers her own question. "She's been asleep most of the day. When she's awake, it isn't for very long, but she knows what's happening."

These two guys – probably in their late 20s or early 30s – are both from Spencer, which is 40 minutes north of Storm Lake. Mom needs to go to Sioux City, which is 70 miles west. Surprisingly, neither of these guys know how to get to Sioux City from here … and neither knows how to get to Mercy Medical Center once they get there.

Seems strange, but I offer to lead the way. The ambulance guys are happy to take me up on the offer.

"How fast should I drive?" I ask.

"You can push it a little bit," one of them responds. "But not TOO much." I nod as if this has made it perfectly clear.

So we leave the hospital in Storm Lake with me driving my 2008 Chrysler 300, leading an ambulance carrying my mother for a 70-minute drive to a hospital in Sioux City. I figure this is the only time in my life I'll be escorting an ambulance anywhere … or at least, I hope that will be the case.

About 35 minutes into the drive, we get on Highway 20, which will take us directly to Sioux City. I turn on my radio for the second time in the last nine days.

Again, I am struck by the song playing. This time it's "I Just Died in Your Arms" by Cutting Crew.

Within five seconds, I turn it off.

Once Mom is in her room at Mercy Medical Center, and all the conversations have taken place with a variety of doctors and nurses, Katie and I are able to spend some time with Mom this evening.

Her back is hurting quite a bit, so Katie and I take turns giving her back massages, which Mom seems to greatly appreciate. We help her with her supper, dabbing her mouth a bit as she's struggling to do some of the things that were so much easier just a few days ago.

For the brief moments she's awake, I read more emails to Mom. And she smiles.

But mostly, she sleeps. Dad, Katie and I visit about the surgery tomorrow, we talk about our kids … and time creeps along slowly.

Around 7 p.m., Dad leaves the room to get something to eat. Mom sits up for me to rub her back. Katie is standing at the foot of the bed, facing Mom.

"Slenderize to genderize," Mom says. "Makes quite a difference."

Katie and I are puzzled. "What did you say Mom?" I ask.

"Slenderize to genderize," Mom repeats. "Makes *quite* a difference!" She says this with a sing-song manner that makes it sound like an old radio ad. Katie smiles at Mom, as I continue to rub her back.

"Oh look," Mom says as she looks around the room. "The angels are coming down…"

"The angels?" Katie asks. "Do you see angels, Mom?"

"Yes, the angels," Mom answers. "I'm ready for my new life."

Katie and I look at each other. We aren't smiling anymore … and our eyebrows are raised. Before we have a chance to say anything more to Mom, or to each other, a doctor walks in the room. This is the third different doctor we've met with today.

I move to the foot of the bed, standing beside Katie as this doctor asks Mom a few questions. Katie and I fill in some blanks as Mom is obviously not completely lucid right now.

The doctor points at me and asks Mom, "Do you know who that man is?"

"Yes," she says.

"Who is he?" asks the doctor.

"That's *Don* Gallagher," Mom answers.

The doctor then points at Katie and asks Mom, "Do you know who that woman is?"

"Yes," Mom answers. "That's *Anne* Gallagher."

I smile as I look at Mom. Her expression is peaceful and happy. She doesn't appear to be in pain. It has been a long, exhausting day for her … and now she looks at Katie and me, and sees herself and Dad standing there side-by-side.

All we can do is hope and pray the surgery tomorrow brings Mom some comfort. If it can help her in some way, it is worth it. Dad, Katie and I all sleep in the room with Mom tonight. It is an especially dark, quiet night. I pray for Mom's angels to bring her some peace and for her surgery tomorrow to be worth the effort.

The Lesson: Take a shot. Mom was never one to shy away from a little risk. She was a confident person who never limited herself based on what others might expect. Mom also didn't ever appear to be afraid of a challenge.

In 1992, Mom became the first full-time leader of the Talented & Gifted (TAG) program in the Storm Lake Community School District. Previously, she taught preschool and kindergarten. Mom was a phenomenal classroom teacher. Running the TAG program would come with new challenges, new strategies and she would begin working with students of all ages. But she was ready for it and excited about it.

When she retired in the spring of 2001, Mom had built a fantastic TAG program in Storm Lake. From the mid-1990s through the rest of her life, she kept close tabs on "her kids" and their successes in life. Mom was proud of their many achievements and it drove her to do her best with that program, which was one of the finest in Northwest Iowa.

CHAPTER 10

WEDNESDAY, JANUARY 7, 2009

Dad, Tim, Katie and I are all in Mom's hospital room with her this morning. Her gall bladder surgery is scheduled for this afternoon. She isn't awake much or for very long. She continues to receive morphine for the pain.

We are all nervous about how Mom will handle the surgery. One of the doctors tells us she will probably need to be on a ventilator for a few days. Looking at her and the frail condition she's in today … it's scary. But we are all still praying for a miracle.

I need to leave early this afternoon, so I can get to Storm Lake in time to pick up Molly and Ben from school.

Mom is asleep as I'm putting my coat on to leave. But then, she opens her eyes. I'm still wearing my glasses as I didn't bother to take the time to put my contacts in today. I walk up to Mom's bed, hold her hand and lean over her.

I can see by her expression she recognizes me.

"I love you," I tell her. "I need to go home and pick up the kids from school. But I'll still be here with you in all my thoughts."

It's hard to explain, but I can see in Mom's eyes that she understands. She always does. Her expression is telling me it's OK for me to leave and that there's no need to apologize. As I'm talking quietly to her, I know she can tell I'm getting emotional … and she gives me a look of support. It's subtle, but I know this is what she's thinking.

"I'll pray for you this afternoon," I say to Mom. "I'll be back tomorrow morning and I'll see you then. Be strong Mom. I love you so much…"

As I bend down to kiss her forehead, my tears are dropping against the lenses of my glasses. In effect, my glasses are keeping my tears from landing on Mom's face. I give her a kiss and squeeze her hand. My fear is this could be *my* good-bye to Mom.

I turn around and Dad is sitting in a chair just a few feet away. I bend over, give him a hug and as his voice is shaking, he says, "You better get out of here before I break down."

I leave the hospital in Sioux City and make the 70-minute drive to Storm Lake. Memories of Mom flood my mind the entire time. I know I will receive a phone call in three or four hours that *could* bring the worst news. But I really don't think that's going to happen. In fact, I am confident that Mom is going to make it through the surgery, the more I think about it.

Why? What makes me think she will get through this?

Because today is Katie's birthday. January 7. Mom will not allow herself to leave us on Katie's birthday. Not a chance.

———————

Around 7 p.m., my phone rings. It's Katie.

She tells me that Mom came through the surgery very well. Katie was with Mom in the recovery room when Mom woke up.

"She opened her eyes, saw me there beside her and the first thing she said was, 'Happy birthday,'" Katie says. "I told her I love her and she said 'I love you' back. She was very lucid for just that brief moment."

———————

At 11:39 p.m., I sent the following email to our list of family and friends:

Just wanted to send you a quick update on how things are going with Mom.

She was transferred from Storm Lake (BVRMC) to Sioux City (Mercy Hospital) yesterday. Mom has been getting a lot of morphine for the pain the last several days and the amount of time that she is awake and aware has become less and less with each passing day.

Today, she had surgery to have her gall bladder removed, as her gall bladder may have been part of the issue with the amount of pain she's been having. At this time, they took a biopsy of her liver, which appears to have quite a bit of cancer.

Prior to today's procedure, the surgeon figured that Mom would likely be on a ventilator for a couple of days following the surgery. However, Mom was already breathing on her own, out of intensive care and back in her room tonight. Hopefully, she will be feeling a little better tomorrow.

I believe the oncologist will speak to us in the morning to let us know what we should expect to happen next.

Finally, I want to thank all of you for your kind words, thoughts and prayers the last couple of weeks. You will never know how much our family appreciates your kindness and support. I have been reading all of the emails to Mom … and she has truly enjoyed each message. All of the wonderful comments and memories bring a smile to her face. She is definitely an incredible person … and we are so blessed to be surrounded by such a tremendous group of family and friends.

Thanks for everything and God bless.

The Lesson: Be strong. Somehow, I knew that Mom would summon the strength to get through that surgery. Today would not – *could not* – be the end. It was Katie's birthday and I truly believe that was one of the reasons Mom pushed through.

Her body was being ravaged by cancer, she was exhausted and in constant pain, but she wasn't complaining. Instead, she opened her eyes and immediately thought of someone else, sharing a "Happy birthday" and an "I love you" with one of her children. It was typical Mom. Full of love. And strength.

The Lesson: Handle loss with grace. This was something Mom had been teaching us for decades. She was a person who had dealt with her share of personal loss through the years, including three miscarriages. She was a rock. I never saw her cry.

One summer day in 1983, our family made a three-hour drive to Adventureland in Altoona, Iowa. All of us, except for Maggie who stayed home, packed into Dad's company van. Our plan was to meet our Uncle Bill (Mom's brother) there and enjoy a couple of days of fun.

We arrived at the Adventureland Inn in the afternoon, where we were going to stay that night after spending the rest of the day at the amusement park. Dad parked in the circle drive and went inside to get us checked in while the rest of us waited in the van.

A few minutes later, Dad came back out of the inn and walked over to Mom's door. He told her that her mother had died … a heart attack. Mom got out of the van and walked inside the inn with Dad. My siblings and I followed them in. We went to a room the Adventureland Inn staff provided to us as a courtesy. Mom's brother Bill was inside and was distraught.

After Mom talked with Uncle Bill for a few minutes, she sat on the edge of the bed in that room and dialed the phone. First, she called her only other sibling, her brother Tom. Then she called Maggie and did the same. Mom remained calm throughout all of it.

"I remember sitting on the edge of a bed while Mom sat on the edge of the other," Katie told me. "We faced each other while I mostly watched her because I was worried about her. And I was sad and scared.

"The whole time, she was composed. At 12 years old, I understood this was her, but it still confused me a little bit. I just accepted it and marveled."

Mom and Uncle Bill drove to Storm Lake together. Dad drove the rest of us back to Strawberry Point. We had to go back home to get what we needed, then drive across the state tomorrow to Storm Lake to prepare for the funeral.

During the time we were at the Adventureland Inn, through the next few days and the funeral, I never saw Mom cry. Looking back, I'm sure she did break down, but she somehow managed to do it privately, out of her children's sight. Someone might argue whether that was necessary or not, but I know that for Mom, it took strength, courage and grace.

She was the person her brother Bill had leaned on, I'm sure she was the person Dad leaned on ... and she was there, in every way, for all of her children during that time.

When I was seven years old, we were assigned to write about our family for our class. Most of my classmates wrote the names, ages and maybe favorite hobbies of their family members. I chose a different route. I wrote about each member of my family and how they reacted when their favorite team lost a game.

It might have been a silly thing to focus on for a young elementary student. But the descriptions were telling ... and Mom loved this paper when it was complete.

I wrote that Dad was a big sports fan and when his favorite team lost a game, he got very upset and yelled at the TV. When my older brothers' favorite teams lost a game, I wrote how angry they became or how long they would be upset.

Mom was a different story. "When my mom's favorite team loses a game, she just slaps her knee and says 'Aw shucks. It's just a game,'" I wrote.

She was always teaching. Some lessons were bigger than others. But every lesson was important then ... and remains meaningful today.

CHAPTER 11

THURSDAY, JANUARY 8, 2009

The temperature is in the single digits this morning, with a biting wind. The sun is shining, though, and the roads are clear as I drive to Sioux City after dropping Molly and Ben off at the elementary school in Storm Lake.

My good friend, Jeff Lucas, stops by Mercy Medical Center this morning to check in on Mom. Jeff was the assistant boys' basketball coach at Storm Lake for four years while I was the head coach. He's a smart guy with a tremendous sense of humor and he would do anything for you.

During the four years Jeff was a teacher in Storm Lake, Mom was running the TAG program. So those two have plenty of common interests, ranging from Storm Lake basketball to the teaching profession to the most recent episode of "Seinfeld."

Currently, Jeff is a guidance counselor at Sioux City East High School. He's aware of Mom's situation through our emails and he has reached out with multiple text messages for updates this week.

Mom thinks very highly of Jeff … and the feeling is mutual. He often refers to her as his "Storm Lake Mom."

Down the hall from Mom's room is a lounge area. When Jeff arrives, this is where he visits with Dad, Tim and me for a few minutes. We talk about the latest high school and college basketball games. Jeff also officiates basketball games and always has a story or two to share. He only has a few minutes before he needs to return to school, so we walk down the hall to see Mom.

We open the door to her room and walk in. Mom is sound asleep in her bed. Maggie and Katie are both in the room too. Jeff walks over to Mom's bed and quietly says a few things to her. Then Jeff tells us he needs to get back to the school and we thank him for coming. I hold the door open as Jeff walks out. I can see he's a bit shaken.

Jeff is only two steps out the door and Mom says, "Hey … that was Jeff Lucas!" She doesn't open her eyes, but she smiles.

I catch Jeff in the hallway and let him know she recognized he was there. I know it means something to him. He tells me he was surprised how she looked, even though he knew her condition. It was still a shock to him.

I thank Jeff again for coming and tell him how much it means to Mom that he came to see her. He walks down the hall and out of sight. The truth is that Jeff's visit meant as much to the rest of us. It was so thoughtful for him to make the effort.

The Lesson: Appreciate your friends. While we were growing up, Mom's best friend was Jackie Jessen, an amazing woman who lived two blocks away with her husband Terry and their seven children. The Jessen kids were roughly the same age as the kids in my family, so Mom and Jackie had plenty in common.

Beyond the large families, though, they were both very intelligent, strong-willed, religious, community leaders with terrific senses of humor.

They were each relied upon in a variety of ways by so many people, but I don't recall ever seeing either of them throwing up their hands and saying, "I can't do this." I'm sure they had tough days, but thankfully, they had each other to confide in and commiserate with.

They both also loved to laugh. When they got together for a cup of coffee – at either our house or the Jessens' – you might not catch what they were saying, but there was no missing their laughter. Mom and Jackie leaned on each other for more than two decades, sharing advice, stories, frustrations and laughter, while keeping each other sane raising a bunch of kids in a small town.

It's remarkable that two of the greatest moms who ever graced the face of the earth ended up living just a couple of blocks from each other. I know that all the Gallagher and Jessen "kids" were lucky, as a result.

Ed makes the two-hour drive to Sioux City for the second time in two days this afternoon. Dad, Maggie, Tim, Katie and I are all with Mom in her hospital room too. She sleeps for almost the entire day and when she's awake, she wants to pray.

The goal of the medical team remains to manage her pain. There is only one outcome now … and it's a matter of *when*, not if. We are all trying to come to terms with this, including Dad. I feel the worst for him. None of this is what any of us expected just two weeks ago. But here we are, sitting in Mom's hospital room, hoping and praying for her to no longer be in pain … and wishing for as much time with her as possible.

Mom just wants to go home. To the hospital in Storm Lake, at least. And given the fact that she's not on a ventilator, the doctors have given the "OK" to send her to Storm Lake tomorrow morning at some point.

———————

The Lesson: Life isn't meant to be fair. Sure, this is a repeat of a lesson I highlighted earlier. But Mom made this point so many times when we were growing up, it's worth a second mention.

Here's another piece from Tim – again from our 2005 Christmas book "Gallagher Family Memories" – that explains this lesson from another angle:

As I thought back to my childhood and teenage years,
I recall Mom saying this: "Life wasn't meant to be fair."
Twenty years later, I began saying it to my children.

What's interesting? I'm not fond of saying it. I doubt she was either.

"Life wasn't meant to be fair" is a quick retort that seeks to get a child off his or her parent's back. The only comeback a child could have is ... well ... there isn't one. And while that makes the saying convenient, it's not enjoyable to use. In fact, I think it was often Mom's last resort. When her explanations and her attempts to appeal to my reasonable sides failed, "life wasn't meant to be fair" was called on as the catch-all summation.

End of conversation.

In the material world, my "life wasn't meant to be fair" mirrors the saying as Mom used it. No, we don't have the nicest clothes. No, we don't have the latest GameBoys. No, we can't spend the month of August seeing the greatest Major League ballparks. No, you cannot go to the R-rated movie of the month.

"Life wasn't meant to be fair."

On a much different and higher level, I learned it's true: "Life wasn't meant to be fair." When classmates shrugged that their parents were rarely, if ever, at their games, I could ask Mom how many strikeouts my class-mate had. When a friend had all the money in the world for a night of doing nothing with nobody, I had 50 cents in my pocket and a mom who would drive me and many siblings to Cedar Rapids to see future

Cub Mark Grace play baseball. When a classmate failed a test because his mother didn't tutor him for hours, I didn't realize it, but it was true: "Life wasn't meant to be fair."

An old teacher liked to say that children spell love this way: T-I-M-E. I know of lots of people my age who didn't enjoy much T-I-M-E at home. I complained then that they got everything else. No, life wasn't fair. Mom was right.

———————

The Lesson: Pray. This is what Mom wanted to do with her final days. Which is not a surprise, really, because she spent so much time praying her entire life. If she wasn't working on making an afghan for someone while she was watching TV, she was saying a rosary.

Mom led rosaries at church for years. The funeral home director would call her routinely to lead rosaries at wakes and funerals.

She taught each of her eight children how to pray ... and until we were school-aged, she would say those prayers together with us. Every night.

During the Lenten season every year we were growing up, Mom would get us out of bed at 6:30 a.m. and we would go to church at 7 a.m. for a half-hour service. Every weekday before school. For us boys, we would serve as altar boys. Five days a week. For six weeks.

Mom was building discipline in us and a respect for our religion. She was also teaching us the importance of prayer.

We attended St. Mary's Catholic Church in Strawberry Point every weekend. Our family always sat in the front pew on the right side of the church. We filled the entire pew on most Sundays. It was a source of pride for Mom, I think. We would always get dressed up and the expectation was that we would behave.

We knew that we would have to sit still in that pew or suffer from Mom's "finger snap."

Nobody in the history of the human race has ever snapped their fingers more loudly than Mom. If we misbehaved in church, she would snap her fingers at a decibel level that made you *certain* it could be heard a few blocks away, maybe even at another church.

I don't remember Mom ever needing to do *more* than that to get us in line. She hardly ever raised her voice at us. But geez, if you heard that "SNAP!" … you knew whatever you were doing was immediately over and done with.

The loudest of her finger snaps were reserved for when we were altar boys. If we ever smirked or messed around up there in front of the entire church … *SNAP!* … and that was it. I think she scared more than a few of my friends with it.

We were to remain respectful at all times when we were in church. And when we prayed. It has stuck with me for all these years.

When you think of one woman keeping six sons and two daughters sitting straight up, behaving and quiet at church – all with the simple snap of her fingers – I'm not sure what's more impressive than that.

When we were at church growing up, you held hands with the people next to you when we recited "The Lord's Prayer." When I held Mom's hand, at the end of the prayer, she would always squeeze my hand three times. I know she did the same thing with my siblings.

I'm not sure Mom and I ever talked about what squeezing my hand three times meant. But in my mind, it was her way of quietly saying, "I love you."

The Lesson: Tend to the sick. This was another area in which Mom was an expert. She had to deal with all kinds of illness and suffering with her children when we were growing up, and she was the greatest. Mom never made you feel like you were troubling her in any way and she could provide you with all the comfort you needed.

That's when you were sick, of course. If you were feeling better, but stretched it out a little to continue getting any "special treatment," she could see through that in a heartbeat. One of her favorite sayings was that "some people are unable to suffer *quietly*" … and it was a dagger.

But if you needed Mom, she was always there. *Always.*

When we were little, if we had to stay home from school because of an illness, Mom would let us spend the day in her bedroom because it had a TV. So on those rare occasions, I remember watching all the game shows that CBS had to offer, with "The Price is Right" usually being the high point.

Mom would bring a little tray with some crackers and a small glass of pop. It was her remedy to settle your stomach.

When I was five years old, I was lying in that double bed, watching that morning's "Showcase Showdown" and I reached over to the nightstand, grabbed the glass of pop … and without sitting up … tipped the glass up to my mouth. Because I was lying down, I just poured Pepsi all over my face, neck and Mom's pillowcase and sheets.

Mom didn't get upset. She calmly got things cleaned up with a towel, changed the sheets, explained my mistake to me and quickly got everything back on track.

I don't know how she was always able to do those things so smoothly and efficiently. It was as if she had been practicing for an event like that for months.

Honesty compels me to report, however, that she wasn't *always* smooth and efficient while tending to the sick.

When I was in my 20s, I had a terrible bout with a kidney stone. It got bad enough that I needed surgery, which was slated to take place at the hospital in Spencer, which is about 40 miles north of Storm Lake. I was in incredible pain and unable to drive. So, Mom offered to take me.

I laid down in the back seat of Mom's 1995 Chevy Lumina. I'm six-foot-two, so it was a tight squeeze. I was on my back with my knees raised. And the pain was excruciating.

As a mother, my mom was *the best*. As a driver, she left a little to be desired. When she learned to drive, she always had her left foot on the brake and her right foot on the gas. This is how she drove her entire life. As a result, a ride with Mom was a little herky-jerky.

Sometimes, a LOT herky-jerky.

On this particular day, while I was hoping for a quick ride to Spencer for my surgery, Mom's feet had other ideas. We would stop … start … stop … start. Then go for a while and then stop … start … stop … start.

It was a constant battle lying there is the back seat, trying to determine what could possibly be happening on the highway to cause all the stopping and starting, while each time the car did either, my pain would sharply increase.

This was just how Mom drove a car.

When we eventually arrived in Spencer, she stopped at a red light so quickly that a football (no idea why there was a football in her car) came tumbling down from above and landed directly in my mid-section. The area I was having the most pain. A direct hit.

It would've been a scene from a sitcom if it hadn't been real.

We did make it to the hospital. The surgery was a success. So that was all good. And I was very grateful to Mom for the ride.

But when it was over, I did ask her if I could drive home.

CHAPTER 12

FRIDAY, JANUARY 9, 2009

Before taking my kids to school this morning, I have a conversation with Tim about how last night went for Mom in the hospital in Sioux City. I sent the following email out to our friends and family at 7:48 a.m.:

Update on Mom...

Last night was a long night for Mom. She had a fever of 102.7 and is still in quite a bit of pain. Her sleep was restless and she mostly just wants to pray.

The plan is to move her today from Mercy Medical Center in Sioux City back to the hospital in Storm Lake, where they will be treating her pain in the time she has remaining. Mom has been very strong throughout all of this, of course.

Dad is doing pretty well, all things considered.

Thank you again for all your kind words, thoughts and prayers. And thank you for the wonderful stories and memories you have shared. Our entire family has been overwhelmed by the outpouring of support and kindness.

Thank you and God bless.

Five of our cousins made the trip across the state to Storm Lake today, arriving around noon. Steve, Mary Lou, Dave, Larry and Bill Gallagher made the long drive on a cold, winter day to come here to see Mom and offer support to our family.

Mom is being transferred today from Sioux City to Storm Lake, but isn't expected to arrive at the hospital here until 1:30 or 2 p.m. Both Dad and Maggie will return to Storm Lake at that time, as well.

Katie had gone back to her home in Cedar Falls yesterday afternoon and drove back to Storm Lake today, so she joins our five cousins and me for lunch. We go to Pizza Hut where we sit together, tell a few stories and share some laughs.

Then, we drive back to the hospital around 1:30 p.m. as Mom is expected to arrive shortly after that time.

Our five cousins, Katie and I visit together in a waiting room on the floor where Mom's new room is located. Shortly after 2 p.m., a nurse comes to tell us the ambulance has arrived with Mom and they will bring her up to her room now. The nurse says she understands Mom was a little agitated on the ride here. She adds that Dad and Maggie drove in a separate car behind the ambulance.

So Katie and I walk out to the hallway, just outside Mom's new room, and wait for her. "Well, of course she was agitated," I say to Katie. "Nobody was with her – no family members anyway – in that ambulance ride."

Katie and I stand there waiting for five or 10 minutes. But to me, it seems to take an hour or more.

Then, the double-doors open as they wheel Mom in her bed into the hallway and toward her room. Katie and I quickly walk up to Mom's bed to see her. Mom's eyes are closed, her head is tilted back and turned to the left a little bit, her mouth is open and her breathing is labored.

"Wait out here while we get her situated and the room set up," one nurse tells us, as she and another nurse enter the room.

I turn to Katie, whose expression has changed from impatient to serious concern.

"There isn't much time," she says to me. "*This is it.*"

Katie has been a social worker previously and worked in a hospice setting. She knows what death looks like. I can tell from her face she has no doubts.

My back rests against the hallway wall opposite Mom's room. We can see there is activity in the room. I'm sure it's productive … I'm sure there are things that need to be done … things that need to be connected, hooked up, verified and so forth. But Mom hasn't had a family member with her in close to 90 minutes.

Time is running short.

Katie calls Maggie on her cell phone to see how far out she and Dad are. Maybe 10 minutes is the answer.

Katie and I are both pacing in small routes in the hallway now. When can we go in and *see her*? What are they DOING in there?

Finally, one of the nurses comes out to the hallway and allows us to go in.

Katie and I walk up to Mom's bed. Katie stands on the left side and I am on the right. Katie holds Mom's right hand, while I hold her left hand. Mom's appearance has changed radically in the last few days and I can see that Katie is right … there is not much time left. This *is* it.

Mom cannot speak, but we are *certain* she knows who we are.

"I love you Mom," I say to her, quietly. "You've been the greatest Mom anyone could ever hope for. We love you so much."

Mom squeezes Katie's hand.

"You gave me everything I needed," Katie tells her. Mom squeezes her hand again.

Each breath Mom takes seems like an effort. Intentional and difficult.

Deep inhale. Exhale. *Pause.* Deep inhale. Exhale. *Pause.*

I look at Katie and say, "She's just waiting for Dad to get here."

Katie nods, then tells Mom, "Dad was right behind the ambulance … he'll be here any minute."

At that moment, the door opens. Dad walks in, with Maggie behind him carrying flowers. They can see what is happening right away. No explanation is needed.

Maggie steps up to the bed on Katie's left. Dad stands on Katie's right. Maggie tells Mom she loves her.

Dad takes Mom's right hand and holds it with both of his.

"We love you," he tells her. "We'll be OK." And then pauses a moment.

Katie puts her right hand on Dad's shoulder and says, "She wants to know that it's OK for her to go, if she's ready to go."

Dad leans forward slightly, holding Mom's hand and says, "It's OK for you to go, if you're ready. We'll be OK. I love you."

At that moment, she takes her final breath.

Mom is gone.

It is 2:42 p.m. on Friday, January 9, 2009.

There are tears for each of the four of us standing around Mom's bed. And hugs. We assure each other that she's no longer in pain and she's undoubtedly in a better place. If there's a Heaven, Mom is surely on her way.

Two minutes later, the door opens. Ed enters. My heart drops for him. Ed's expression is full of sadness and pain as he walks to Mom's bed.

"She's at peace now," Dad tells Ed and they hug. Maggie, Katie and I each give Ed a hug. Then he stands next to her bed and holds her hand as tears roll down his cheeks.

There is extreme sadness looking at Mom in the bed. But also relief. She had been through so much. She had fought with all her heart and gave everything she had. It was time.

It strikes me now that we have five cousins in a waiting room just down the hall. They are expecting to come see Mom and give her some support. "I'll go tell the cousins," I say to Katie, who nods through her tears.

I open the door to leave the room as a nurse enters. I walk down the hallway and into the waiting room. Steve, Mary Lou, Dave, Larry and Bill are visiting, but they stop abruptly when I enter. They can see it on my face, I think. "I'm so sorry," I say to them. "She's gone." We share hugs and I tell them how much we appreciate them making the trip.

Then I walk back down the hallway to Mom's room.

Dad, Maggie, Katie, Ed and I gather around Mom's bed and quietly say a few prayers. Father Bruce Lawler, the priest at St. Mary's Church in Storm Lake, is making the rounds at the hospital this afternoon and enters the room.

The six of us say the "Lord's Prayer" together. Father Lawler shares a few comforting words for us.

I look at the clock. It's almost 3 p.m. I need to go to the elementary school to pick up Molly and Ben.

"I've got to pick up the kids," I say to Dad and give him another hug. And for the first time in my 39 years, I go out into the world without Mom as a part of it.

I park my car about a block from the elementary school. I walk down the sidewalk, across the street and up to the playground area. It's another bitterly cold winter day. The students are just coming out the doors. The noise, the talking, the laughter … these are the sounds my mom heard every day of her professional career as a teacher. She must have loved that sound.

As I'm looking for Molly and Ben in the crowd of students running out into the playground in their coats, hats, gloves and boots, one of the school's teachers – who happens to be my parents' next-door neighbor – walks up to me and asks, "How is your mom doing? I heard she's in the hospital."

"I'm sorry Carol," I reply. "She actually just passed away about a half-hour ago." Carol offers her sympathy and prayers … and I continue looking for the kids.

Ben finds me and together, we find Molly. I hold their gloved hands as we walk to the car.

When they are both buckled in the back seat, I turn around from the front seat to face them. I tell them Grandma Gallagher went to Heaven today. As they begin to cry, I tell them she wouldn't want them to be sad. "She loves you both very much," I say. "Now, she loves you from her place in Heaven."

They're bright kids. They'll have their questions. But for now, they have their sadness. Molly and Ben know they will miss their grandma. They spent so much time with her.

My hope is they will always remember the special relationship they had with Grandma Gallagher.

At 6:26 p.m., I send the following email to our list of family and friends:

Mom passed away this afternoon at the hospital in Storm Lake.

She was transferred from Sioux City to Storm Lake by ambulance early this afternoon and the ambulance personnel said that she was a bit agitated on the ride. When they wheeled her into her room, Katie and I were here waiting for her. The nurse said that once we went in to see her, Mom calmed right down. Katie and I spoke to Mom and held her hands. She knew who we were and could hear us, but was not able to speak.

Then, we told her that Dad was only a few minutes away. It was clear to us that this was all she was waiting for.

When Dad came into the room, he held Mom's hand, told her that he loves her ... and that it was OK for her to go. And just like that, she was gone.

It was a beautiful, peaceful end to an incredible, wonderful life on this earth. And as Mom said a couple of nights ago, "I am ready to start my new life."

Again, we would like to send our tremendous gratitude to all of you for your great friendships throughout the years and your enormous support, thoughts, memories and prayers the past couple of weeks. Thank you from the entire Gallagher Family. We are lucky to have you in our lives. And we are grateful that Mom is now at peace in Heaven.

The Lesson: Love always wins. Mom managed to teach a final lesson, waiting for Dad to arrive at the hospital in Storm Lake. She kept herself alive, without question, to give Dad a chance to say good-bye. She willed herself to remain with us, giving each of her children the peace of knowing she was ready to go.

Mom's love for Dad and her family was enough to give her that incredible strength. She knew this moment would be *that* meaningful to all of us.

Even with her last breath – just as she had done for our entire lives – Mom taught a lesson that would stick. Love is more powerful than anything. Even death.